20 Tough Questions Teenagers Ask

And 20 Tough Answers

20 Tough Questions Teenagers Ask

Questions

Teenagers

Ask

And 20
Tough Answers

Lois Leiderman Davitz, Ph.D. & Joel R. Davitz, Ph.D.

Paulist Press
New York / Mahwah, N.J.

Cover and text design by Cynthia Dunne

Copyright © 1998 by Lois Leiderman Davitz

LIBRARY OF CONGRESS CATALOGING-IN-PUBLICATION DATA
Davitz, Lois Jean.
20 tough questions teenagers ask and 20 tough answers / by Lois Leiderman Davitz, Joel R. Davitz.
    p.   cm.
Summary: A compilation of questions and answers based on issues of importance especially to teenagers, including sexuality, faith, death, contraception, divorce, emotional health, and family relationships.
    ISBN 0-8091-3807-7
    1. Teenagers—Miscellanea—Juvenile literature. 2. Adolescent psychology—Miscellanea—Juvenile literature. 3. Parent and teenager—Miscellanea—Juvenile literature. 4. Teenagers—Religious life—Miscellanea —Juvenile literature. [1. Teenagers. 2. Adolescence. 3. Parent and teenager. 4. Teenagers—Christian life.] I. Davitz, Joel Robert. II. Title.
HQ796.D34   1998
305.235—dc21   98-18813
                                                     CIP
                                                      AC

Published by Paulist Press
997 Macarthur Boulevard
Mahwah, New Jersey 07430

Printed and bound in the
United States of America

Contents

20 Tough Questions Teenagers Ask

And 20 Tough Answers

Teenagers like yourselves have tough questions that you rarely get a chance to ask. It's not all that simple to confront adults with straightforward, right-to-the-point questions about such topics as sex, drugs, faith and contraception, just to mention a few sensitive issues everyone faces some time or another in life. Shyness, embarrassment, fears about being judged or making parents or other adults angry and uncomfortable probably keep you from bringing up these kinds of personal matters.

And that's why this book came into being. We're going to face these tough questions. There will be no backing off. We went right to the teens themselves, inside and outside of the United States, and asked them to speak to us in their own voices. And, in return, we have suggested some tough, down-to-earth, no-nonsense, meaningful responses that we feel will make a real difference in the way you feel about yourself.

There will be no preaching. There are no sets of rules to memorize, no dos and don'ts. Rather, the goal is to present *rational* responses, *ways* to think about right or wrong, and *moral values.* The responses and opinions in this book are meant to give you enough room to work out your own answers to these questions. We know that you know your own situation best and that there is no one perfect response. Wisdom that is your own ultimately comes from naming and owning your own values and beliefs and from your way of construing the world in which you live.

In preparing these twenty tough questions we are deeply

indebted to two groups: First, to the teenagers who anonymously asked the questions, and second, to the clergy, nuns, teachers, guidance counselors, parents, psychologists and teenagers themselves who cooperated in providing insights and guidance that are the foundation for the responses.

Lois Leiderman Davitz, Ph.D.
Joel R. Davitz, Ph.D.

20 Tough Questions Teenagers Ask

And 20 Tough Answers

The tough question:

"Should I have sex before getting married?"

"I'm not afraid of having sex with my boyfriend. He's the one holding back. I can't understand why. If two people are in love, isn't sex right and beautiful?"

Caroline
Seventeen years old
Major interests: My boyfriend, church youth group; field hockey; social studies; where I'm going to college.

"My boyfriend and I have been going steady now for over a year. My parents have met him. I don't want him coming over too much 'cause my mom is against my going steady, though it seems funny, because she got married when she was young. Right now I've no intentions of getting married, but it's interesting that my mom was on her own with a husband when she wasn't that much older than me— maybe about five years or so.

"Back to my boyfriend problem. We love each other. It isn't like we just met and said we were in love. It's taken time. You can't imagine how I feel being with him. We spend as much time as we can together. He's into sports a lot so he has practice and I always hang around and wait for him. We don't even have to do a lot to be happy in each other's company. Sometimes we'll just take a walk or hang out at a mall. What I'm trying to say is we don't have to spend a lot of money to have fun or anything like that. It's being together that counts.

"We talk a little about marriage; we know it's going to happen someday. He doesn't have to ask me. It's something you sort of know because he is exactly who I want to spend the rest of my life with.

"It's not that we plan on this right away. His folks want him to go to college. They would feel terrible if he didn't. Both of them went to college, so that's not an issue. It's the same way with me. I'm not stopping my education after high school. Everybody knows nowadays you have to have all the education you can get. But I thought that if we went to the same college we could live together. We talk a lot about plans for the kind of life we want some day.

"The problem now is sex. Right now we do everything *but*; it's frustrating, and it's got to be the same for him. I can tell it's hard for him because after we're together like that he gets on edge and so do I. Sometimes it just spoils everything—the holding back, I mean.

"I can't see that sex is all wrong. I honestly have a problem with that idea. We love each other. We plan on marriage. What can be so wrong in our having sex? If two people like us are in love, isn't sex *right and beautiful?* It's not that either of us has had sex before. I am a virgin. I would rather lose my virginity with him than anyone else, and that alone shows my love. It's not a matter of him not loving me. I know that. He's holding back because he's afraid of what his mom would say if she found out. But how would she find out? I can't even bring up the subject of sex without my mom going bananas. I'm sure it's no different in his family.

"I told him if we had sex, that would show our *real commitment* to each other. We're not children. I look a lot older than seventeen, and so does he. I think we are mature and I agree that sex is wrong for most kids. It really is. But with mature people like ourselves, having sex would be different. It would be an expression of our love. It makes me unhappy when he tells me his mom would kill him if she found out how serious we are.

"My parents don't know about us. I think that's better. They're from another generation. They don't understand that kids today are different from kids in their day. I don't want to hurt my parents, but it would be impossible for them to understand where I'm coming from now with my boyfriend. There comes a time in life when kids have to cut loose from parents and make their own decisions."

> *"Sex is on my mind. I don't do drugs. I don't drink.*
> *I think about sex. Sometimes it's very painful, and I*
> *feel confused. What is so wrong about premarital*
> *sex?"*
>
> Jimmy
> Sixteen years old
> Major interests: Sex; getting better grades in school;
> track team (hope to be captain someday).

"I never had a girlfriend before. I wasn't interested, and then it happened to me bam-sudden. I can remember exactly how and where it happened. It was at school, after track practice. I was headed to the locker room. She was standing there watching squirrels and laughing. She was all alone, and she was laughing at the way they were chasing around. I watched too, but I didn't think about the squirrels. She's got this long hair and it was pulled back, so I could see her whole face. I mean, I had never seen her before. I couldn't believe she went to my school. She was in my class—the same year.

"I always thought it would be hard to talk to girls. It's easy, you know, to kid around, make smart-aleck remarks. With her it wasn't like that at all. We talked about school and not really much of anything. It was so easy. When I had to go change, I wanted to ask her to wait for me, but I was afraid. I ran like hell, and I couldn't believe it when I came back and she was waiting, sitting on the stone fence.

"That's the way it's been. We don't have to say something all the time. From day one, we always knew what the other was thinking. That first day, I walked her home. She doesn't live far from where I live, which surprised me because I'd never seen her before. I swear I never had laid eyes on her, so it wasn't like all this was planned.

"My mom is pretty sharp. She looked at me when I came

into the house and asked me what happened. I said 'Nothing,' but she accused me of trying to fool her. It's like she has radar or something. She always knows when something is up.

"So I made up some story about a test. We always have tests, so it wasn't like I was putting her on with a lie, but it's not something you tell a parent. How do you say that I talked, really talked, to a girl for the first time? Besides, I was feeling pretty excited myself.

"We've been going together for six months. It's been steady. My parents still don't know. They know I met some girl and I was thinking about taking her to the junior prom. But that's all there is. Her folks are strict so she can only go out a couple of times a week, but she has to be home by ten thirty. We spend every minute that we can together—lunchtimes, between classes. Sometimes after school she'll wait for me until practice is over.

"The other guys know what's going on, but they know better than to say anything because of the way I feel about Allison. I guess it's that my friends don't joke about girls they really like. The only time it's that kind of talk is when the guys aren't really in love with the girls.

"I think my mom has some idea but my dad could care less. He's not into talking about my social life. I'd like to talk to my mom about sex but I can't bring myself to do it. Besides, I don't think she'd want me to. My mom is like that. I've hinted to her and she's backed off and basically shut me up before I could even begin.

"The other evening, Allison and I were talking on the phone before we went to sleep. We fell asleep talking to each other. My mom told me she came into my room and took the phone from my hand. It's been hell on the two of us. We're both against premarital sex but that's not the problem. The problem is that there's a big difference between believing and something happening.

"Some of the guys have had sex. I know that for a fact.

I'm not the kind of guy who's out for one-night stands. With me, an evening of just sex without anything else is all wrong. Sex for me has to have something more—that is, it has to be with a girl like Allison, who means something. I'm worried it's going to happen. I fight my desire, but sometimes I can't take the physical pain.

"Allison doesn't do anything, believe me, to make me want to push her into sex. She's not that kind. I know she's never had another boyfriend. She doesn't have to tell me how she feels. I know she would like sex, too. It shouldn't happen, but I'm worried that it will.

"I don't know how to handle the pain, the desire, and that's why I need someone to tell me what to do. My mom can't help me, for sure. What do I do? I'm left with a lot of physical pain, desires and thoughts about sex, and it gets me down. When that happens, I put on my stereo headset and blast my head with music. It's better to go deaf, I figure, than have the pain.

"I don't want to lose her. I feel kind of desperate because I love her very much. Funny how I think about the future and I see myself going faster and faster, and there's Allison at the finish line and we have sex. If that happens, it is the right thing for both of us, isn't it?"

The tough answer:

We're going to respond to Jimmy and Caroline together. It's interesting, isn't it, that kids and even adults, we're sure, forget that both boys and girls can struggle with the same conflicts, the same kinds of desires in more similar ways than either sex would realize.

But let's get back to the tough question about sex before marriage. And this is a tough question. In fact, we would rank the question you've both raised as pretty high on our list of tough questions. First of all, both of you are so right about many of the points you noted. Caroline, when you asked that if two people are in love, isn't *sex right and beautiful,* you were right on target. There's a little *more* to it, as we'll talk about later, but you are undeniably right in this comment.

And Jimmy, when you talked about the physical pain of desire reaching almost a breaking point with you, we would again agree—how *right* you are. Sexual desire is undeniably one of the most powerful feelings that anyone can experience, which is why we said at the beginning that any discussion about sex ranks near the top of our list of tough questions and answers.

However, we disagree strongly with you, Caroline, about your now being old enough to cut loose and make a decision regarding whether or not to have sex because you feel and look mature. Of course you are mature, a lot more mature than you were at ten years of age. You may even look a lot older than your age. But don't discount some of the wisdom your parents may possess.

By the way, it may be of interest to you both that your parents are no different from countless other parents who back off from discussing sex with their kids. Teenager after teenager has told us that they *wish* their parents would talk about sex. Unfortunately, the vast majority of parents kind of hope that their kids will learn about sex, but certainly not in the context of an after-dinner discussion in the home. They often play ostrich, wanting to believe that sexual desires don't exist. But do understand, Jimmy and Caroline, that for your parents, talking about intimate sexual experiences with their kids probably makes them very uncomfortable. They may feel this way because, after all, *both of you represent the fulfillment of their own sexual experiences.* So, just for a moment, let's say, "OK, parents are parents, and it's easier to talk to them about a baseball game or the upcoming prom than about sex."

Now, let's go back to what you said, Caroline. If two people are in love, isn't sex right and beautiful? The answer is, without any hesitation—of course it is right and beautiful. Sometimes this idea is completely lost on a lot of people, but we're not going to worry about that now. However, and this is a big "however," sex is right and beautiful when the time and place and purpose are all in the proper configuration. Let us give you an example. A marriage ceremony is right and beautiful. I think that both of you would agree to that. However, *if* the marriage ceremony takes place, let's say, in a gym locker room, it could still be right for the people involved because they are very much in love, but it could hardly, by anyone's standards, be called beautiful.

By the same token, *if* a marriage ceremony takes place in a beautifully decorated church, without any expense spared for flowers, dress, tuxedos, food or presents, but the two people are less than thrilled and **not** in love, that marriage ceremony could be beautiful but hardly right. The point we are making is that *"right" and "beautiful"* **must go together, and this means appropriate** *in both the time and the place in one's life.*

Caroline, you mention that your boyfriend is holding back, while you feel the sexual act would show his commitment. This may or may not be the case. Besides, one has to think of what you mean by *commitment.* For a moment we'll assume that by *commitment* you mean "remaining faithful." Being faithful in high school, while you're both students, is one thing. Being faithful throughout a lifetime, with a family and responsibilities, is another story.

The reality is that people change, and, with rare exceptions, the feelings one has at sixteen may very well not be the feelings one has at sixty. Jumping into an early commitment before you've even graduated from high school and know who you are, where you are going or what either of you will be doing in the future, is a pretty big order. In saying this we don't, for a moment, want to put down or dismiss your feelings of being in love. At this moment, we *know* that the love you have for each other is real and something that you both share and enjoy.

Then, you may ask, why not sex, which you feel will represent the completion of the feelings you have for each other. Jimmy, this also applies to you. You make it pretty clear that you really hold this girlfriend of yours in high esteem. Those sentiments come through loud and clear. You don't want to use her just to satisfy your own desires. *But*—and there's a lot of weight resting on this *but*—holding off on the sex as an expression of your affection *is* a *given*. Sex without any reservations is an expression of love, and part of the purpose of this love is to have children. That's what marriage is all about.

Desire, the physical pain you are experiencing—and we know exactly what you are talking about—can get in the way of enjoying each other's company. It's as if you can't see the forest because of the trees, as the old cliché says. You are focusing on sexual activity and forgetting all the fun that the two of you might have in the day-to-day sharing of each other's company.

Is this fair? you could reasonably ask. We can't really answer that. Fair? Would it be fair if the two of you have premarital sex and then in six months have a knock-down-drag-out argument and split? Would it be fair if the two of you married now, had a child and became school dropouts, struggling to support a family that you both would, in time, grow to resent? I'm sure, given your intentions to go on to school, that the consequences of having a child would prevent you from achieving your goals and result in resentment. Would it be fair to the child you brought into the world? Would it be fair to your parents, who may have to struggle to support this extra family?

There is a right time and a right place, as we said a little while back. And timing is everything in life. Resorting to a furtive sexual experience because you both have to make sure your respective sets of parents don't find out is probably not beautiful. Repeated furtive sexual experiences with the threat of pregnancy looming over your heads is also probably not the ideal way to show love and commitment. The blunt truth is that premarital sexual experiences do have a component of furtiveness and guilt. Is that fair to any of you?

We know you probably are going to counter with, "What about contraception?" which is another tough question that we'll deal with in a later section. There's always a risk no matter what. On the one hand, we could say to you, "OK, go for it—get your sexual gratification because you'll have fun." Perhaps your immediate gratification might be resolved. But would this resolve the *bigger* issue of the meaning and purpose of marriage and the sexual act? Definitely not!

We just can't dismiss the fact that the sexual act, a beautiful and right sexual act, has a right time and a right place in an individual's life. ***When all of the pieces go together—the initial love, marriage vows, commitment—the sexual act performed for its true purpose will be right and beautiful.*** It's never going to be right and beautiful in the back seat of an automobile and it's never going to be right and beautiful taking place furtively in a gym locker room. No one is going to be happy in the long run—not you, your parents or anyone who comes into your life at another time.

The tough question:

"Why can't my parents respect my privacy?"

"If my mom and dad knew about my girlfriend, they'd yell bloody murder. They'd never let me see her again. I think kids have to hide certain things from their parents. That's the way life has to be."

Martin
Seventeen years old
Major interests: Soccer; steady girlfriend; where I'll go to college.

"My parents want to know everything about me. I get grilled. They know all about my girlfriend, not from me, but from someone who lives next door to my girlfriend who knows someone who knows my mom. I don't think it's right. I want some things in my life to be private. If I ever was stupid enough to bring her home to meet my parents, they would rake her over the coals with questions. I really need some space and some privacy. I don't want them in every part of my life."

"It's not fun being sixteen and turning into a perpetual liar. My parents want to know every little thing about me—even the smallest detail. I really resent having to report like this. I have no privacy."

Lisa
Sixteen years old
Major interests: Glee club; my piano lessons; improving my grades.

"Its got so that I only walk in the house and my parents start jumping all over me about where I've been and what I'm doing. Most of the time they are really great, so I feel guilty talking like this.... But there are some things I don't want to tell them, so I end up making up stories to make them happy. That's what I mean when I said I'm turning into a perpetual liar."

> *"It really is getting to me—not being able to share*
> *things with my parents the way I did before. Now*
> *they want to know too much. I'm beginning to hide*
> *things from them, like what I read, movies, TV pro-*
> *grams, mostly girls and dating. I need my own*
> *space."*
>
> *Timothy*
> *Seventeen years old*
> *Major interests: Soccer; band; getting good grades.*

"Everything's kind of changed. I guess some of it's my fault. I always told my mom a lot of things that happened. Now I don't want to anymore. I don't think I should tell her because she gets upset if she doesn't like what I'm saying. I wish I could talk to my parents about what I'm doing. Then again, I don't really want to. I think some things in my life are my business—not theirs. I feel guilty hiding a lot."

> *"I know why my folks took the phone out of the*
> *room. They didn't like the idea of not hearing what*
> *I was saying. They want to know every detail."*
>
> *Madeline*
> *Fifteen years old*
> *Major interests: Improving my grades; being appreci-*
> *ated by my friends; getting a boyfriend.*

"It really bothers me that they won't let me have a phone in my room anymore. I know why they took it out. They gave some silly excuse, but they resent my having all these people to talk to. My mom is dying to hear me on the phone. She's like a shadow when I'm home. Oh, not that bad, but like she wants to know so much stuff. I don't feel I have any privacy, and I'm old enough not to have her on my back all the time."

The tough answer:

Sound familiar? Invasion of privacy? Too many questions? Parents who are unable to leave you alone? Stories you make up just to please them? Having you report in as if you were six instead of sixteen? We have an idea that this list of gripes about parental invasion of your privacy is like the tip of an iceberg.

More than anything else, teenagers like yourselves resent parents hanging over their every word, watching their every action, monitoring phone calls and checking on their friends. We agree that it's hard to keep one's cool when this happens. On occasion, parents do step over the boundaries of their teenagers' private space.

In responding with our tough answer, we have to walk a fine line and do our best not to take sides. Let's begin with parents. By the time a parent has a teenager, they have some experience to draw upon. And yet, nothing shocks a parent more than suddenly having a teenager around the house. The little child is gone. In his or her place is a very different sort of person. Most parents, whether they admit it or not, are taken aback with this "almost adult" in their midst. They may even think to themselves, "Why, it was only yesterday that my daughter [or my son] was a little preschooler." Frankly, it's not so easy to one day be the parent of a child and the next to be the parent of an adult.

What does this all mean? It means that parents who are used to being in charge, arranging and planning for their children, used to making all sorts of pronouncements about life, suddenly must change the way they behave. That's precisely the time when problems develop. *Parents simply can't change fast enough to suit their kids.*

For example, when a six-year-old comes home from a birthday party, parents are used to asking a "million" questions about the color of the cake, the games played and the friends who were there. However, when a sixteen-year-old comes home from a party and gets the same kind of questioning, there's resentment. What games were played? (Are you kidding?) Who was there? What did you drink? Then their teenager storms out of the room yelling something about resenting being grilled with questions.

Why do parents question? In part, they question because they want to make sure everything is OK in their children's lives. Parents do worry. The world outside the home is not as uncomplicated as it was years ago. Drugs and alcohol, just to name a few possible problems represent *realistic risks*, and caring parents are concerned and are justified in these concerns. So, when a teenager comes home at dawn on a Saturday "night," and the parents are chewing their fingernails and pacing the kitchen floor, it's inevitable that they will bombard a daughter or a son with questions. You have to understand where parents are coming from.

Now let's look at your side. All those questions, all those prying comments are embarrassing, uncomfortable, disturbing and often irritating. From your point of view, it's an invasion of your privacy, an unacceptable grilling about personal affairs. After all, you probably say to yourself, "I don't check on where they're going or what they're doing. It's not fair that they want to know everything that I'm doing."

"You must be joking," Madeline might say, "if you think taking a telephone out of my room is a way of caring. It sounds more like prying than caring."

We don't agree with you, Madeline. Chances are, your parents were worried about your school work, concerned about your doing well, and hoping that you are living up to your potential. They may have felt that you spent far too much time on the phone, and not enough time on your school assignments. Was this the best way for them to handle the situation? Perhaps not. They might have over-reacted. On occasion, we all do. Parents are human. Caring may make them do or say things that appear to be uncaring—for example, exploding when a teenager returns home at some ungodly hour or hangs out with known troublemakers.

It's important that we discuss how some of these situations might be handled. Don't forget that we totally support your right to privacy, as long as you aren't in trouble, are making a sincere effort in school and are not involved with drugs or alcohol or engaged in any other dangerous activities. You absolutely have a right *not* to be under a microscope.

On the other hand, parents, *too*, have rights, and one of their rights is freedom from worry—feeling secure in the knowledge that their kids are not messing up their lives or flirting with trouble. They deserve to know that their kids are headed in the right direction in life.

Given these *rights* on both sides—and you must admit they're fair—what can you reasonably do to insure your privacy? As teenagers, you feel that you want to take charge of your own lives. That's what adults do. Therefore we're going to urge you to be patient and behave in an adult way. You're going to take the lead and teach your parents, because parents really are teachable.

We would like to see teenagers take the initiative. For example, let's say that you have parents interested in everything that goes on in your life to the point of making you angry. Address their fears and concerns. Why not volunteer enough information to ease their anguish? For example, if you're dating a girl, and your dad wants to know all about the girl, you might tell him to trust your judgment, the girl is in your class. You might tell him her name or anything else that you feel is important for him to know. Let your mom in on some details too. Let her know enough about the girl so that she is comfortable with the person her son is dating. Parents are all naturally curious and protective.

Each of you knows what 'bugs' your parents. In one family it might be a fear of alcohol; in another, drugs; in still another, gangs who get into trouble. The more you can reassure parents that they have no cause to worry, the better your chances are for a good relationship. If, on the other hand, you are getting into drugs, be grateful for their concerns and take any help they can give you to kick the habit. If you are drinking and your parents find out, be thankful that they care enough about you to check your behavior before you wrap a car around a tree. Consider the alternative—if you continue headlong on a course of dangerous habits, you may not live long enough to even object to their concerns.

You all need your parents' interest and support, and they, in turn, need your reassurance that your lives are going well. Each of you told us you resent, more than anything, being treated like a little kid. We understand your resentment. But if you want to be treated like an adult, then you have an obligation to behave like one. Translated into everyday behavior, this means that if Dad or Mom asks a sensitive question, don't slam the door and walk out of the room. Act like an adult. In a straightforward manner, explain to your parents what has been going on in your life.

Back to the girlfriend you're afraid your mom and dad would question. You might tell your parents that you'd be happy to bring her around, but would they please not bombard her with questions. Explain that your girlfriend will feel uncomfortable. Mention that they, too, would get uncomfortable if, on a first meeting, someone asked them the cost of their home, their income and so forth. In other words, set the ground rules for the interaction.

Families are going to differ; that is, parents will be more or less intrusive into the private lives of their children depending upon their level of concern. We think each of you has a pretty good idea of what worries your folks and what drives them to do a lot of questioning and invade your privacy. For one family, the issue may be pregnancy— the fear that their daughter may become pregnant or that their son will get a girl pregnant. Such an event could devastate a family. Your parents may need reassurances in order to ease their tensions.

It's important never to lose sight of your parents' motivation for invading your space or intruding upon your private world. Their motivation mainly stems from sincere concern, and your determined efforts to share with them and reassure them will be an important step toward adulthood, freedom and finally, the enjoyment of your own personal right to privacy.

The tough question:

"Is it wrong just to try some drugs?"

"Drugs are taking over my life. I feel sometimes like I'm watching myself, outside my own body, seeing myself deteriorate. Drugs are taking over my life."

Robert
Fifteen years old
Major interests: Not much of anything except drugs.

For several years, Robert, a gifted musician, has been lead drummer in a rock group composed of high school seniors. Although the "baby" of the group, his talents equal the skills of much older players. But, despite his musical talent, Robert has gradually lost interest in music. In fact, he admits that he isn't much interested in anything any more—a fact he attributes to his increased use of drugs.

"I'm not a fool. I know what's happening. That's the queer part of it all; it's like I'm two people. I'm not much interested in anything. Before the music, I liked sports. Now, not much counts with me. My parents would never understand. If they ever got any idea of what's happening to me, it would break the whole family apart. That's for sure. My mom couldn't take it, I know that. That's why I have to hide a lot from her. If she ever found out, she'd be sick. My mom sees me as some kind of golden boy. That's how she talks about me. She's always bragging to everyone. She told my aunt that I am so great. I get sick to my stomach when I hear her 'cause I know it's a big, fat lie.

"It started so easy. This friend of mine and I smoked some pot, and I didn't get sick or anything, like some kids. It was my first time smoking, and I didn't like it really. I don't know why I continued. Maybe it was because of one friend. I kind of looked up to him, and so I wouldn't let on that I didn't see what the big deal was. I thought I'd fool around and then quit. It started with just a little here and there. I've tried to stop, but it doesn't work. And I don't even like it. That's what's so funny. I hate it.

"Maybe what I mean is I hate myself and I can't stop. I keep doing it, day after day after day. I don't know how to stop. I don't know if I want to stop. What will I do if I do stop?

"Sometimes I'm sitting in class and my eyes start to feel stiff; my eyelids get heavy, and I blink, trying to stay awake. I've rubbed my eyes red, and it hurts when I do this. My eyes get sore. You know, there are times when I wish someone would see what's happening to me, like a teacher or something. I don't understand why my parents don't see it. They've never said anything to me. My mom has even said to me, "Robert, I'm glad you don't use drugs." I can't believe she's for real. I mean doesn't she know? Maybe she doesn't want to know, I guess.

"Drugs are taking over my life, and I can't do anything about it. I want to stop. That's what I tell myself. Then again I'm not so sure. What will I have left? You know, for so long now all I've thought about is drugs, getting my highs. If I let go, what will happen to me?"

The tough answer:

Robert, you're lucky. You're lucky because you are intelligent. You're not stupid. You're lucky because you're at the stage when you can see what's happening to you. You're lucky because you're at a point where you are able to ask for help. But first, let's be straight with you. You aren't alone with your drug problem. When we surveyed teenagers about tough questions in their lives, we were surprised to discover how many brought up the issue of drugs as the number one problem. Some of the kids asked for help for a friend. Others admitted it was their problem. Admitting that there is a problem is a giant step toward working out a solution.

You talk about losing interest in everything. Yes, that is a consequence of drugs, but let's backtrack a bit. You probably began with a dare, pressure from a friend, as you said. It doesn't matter how it happened. What *did* happen was that at some point you felt thrills and excitement—the sensation of flirting with danger. There was a high feeling. You felt a certain bravado because you were doing something pretty dangerous. We understand how you felt. You're human. Everyone wants to feel different and daring.

Maybe up until that point you were the good kid, the "golden boy" your mother talks about. Breaking out made you feel like a big shot outside of the home. That's the beginning, but don't kid yourself. Once you are hooked, it isn't just thrills alone that keep someone taking drugs. Your mind can say *no*, but your body craves the drug. ***Actual physical changes occur in your body***. Now we don't know, of course, what physical changes, if any, may have occurred with you, but if you are addicted, you don't have much of a choice. Your body will demand drugs and your life will quickly go into downhill skid.

Don't kid yourself. You no longer have a choice. Deciding how much drugs to take and when you will take them will no longer be in your control. Your body will be in the driver's seat—not your mind. That sounds pretty strong but it's the truth. It's not like an urge to buy a chocolate bar; if you don't get the chocolate bar you can survive. Drug addiction isn't a piece of chocolate. Your body will want that drug so badly that you'll do anything to stop the craving. The rest of the world be damned. You'll want that drug badly and will need it quickly.

That's why you're going to need special help. You can't stop or handle a drug problem by yourself, and you can't be master of your desires anymore. ***You must get help from specialists***. We know that kids sometimes say they can quit anytime they want to, but they're only fooling themselves. One recovered addict described the experience of his body "screaming" to be satisfied and his mind trying to break the habit without success. For this intelligent man, the horror was seeing himself do anything for drugs just because of the physical demands of his own body. As he put it, "Being out of control was hell."

Pep talks on our part won't change your behavior. Taking vows to stop; making promises all over the place; heartfelt pleas from your parents—none of these will really work when a body is addicted to drugs and the craving sets in. That's what kids sometimes fail to realize. It's a time for professional help. Getting rid of a drug habit requires experienced counselors. It's going to take time, but it can and will happen. The reason we're confident in cases like yours is because you *want* to change and you're young enough to change. Getting "grooved" again in a different way of life *is* possible.

You ask what you will have left in your life if you give up drugs. We say if you continue to use drugs ***you won't have a life***. It's as simple as that. Are we trying to scare you? Yes, Robert, that's exactly what we're doing, and let us tell you why. We'd like to tell you about two teenagers like yourself whose "stories" are forever imprinted on our minds.

One was a lovely looking girl, a dancer, full of life and fun. She didn't have a sixteen-year-old birthday party like her friends. Instead, we accompanied her parents to the hospital where she lay in a crib, huddled over in a fetal position, whimpering. She had taken drugs in such quantities that all of her controls were gone. There is no happy ending to her story. She remains hospitalized, hands tied so she can't pull her hair out and hurt herself. She was going to show everybody and refused all help.

Our second story is about a talented seventeen-year-old boy with lots of promise in his life. He, too, found drugs a source of high pleasure, a way of proving he was one of the "in" group that he chose to hang out with at school. We were with his parents when they visited him in a padlocked cell covered with a blanket, his mind strung out on drugs. We'd like to report a happy ending to his case too, but we can't. He refused to give in and accept help.

Oh yes, you say, we're being very obvious, aren't we, by telling you horror stories. ***You know, sometimes the obvious things in life turn out to be truths***. You've got to be scared, Robert. And other kids like yourself, hooked on drugs, have to be scared. You can't say, "It won't happen to me." You can't say, "I'll never be slobbering, cowering in the corner of a cell or huddled in a crib." The real truth, the real drama that plays out is that continued use of drugs spells this kind of end. For some it will happen later; for others it will turn out to be sooner.

That's why, the tough, straight answer we have to tell kids like yourself is while you *still* have a mind, *get help*. When the mind goes, as it inevitably does with drugs, you won't be able to do anything about your condition. If you were already a hard-core addict or a lot older, we wouldn't even dream of giving you this kind of answer. But we feel that, with teenagers, there's still a fighting chance for them to take charge of their lives *with* help. And this means letting your parents, a counselor at school or any other responsible adult know about your problem so you can be properly directed to a drug center for rehabilitation.

4

The tough question:

"I don't like the way I look. What can I do about that?"

"I would give anything in the world to have a pretty face and a body to match."

Francine
Fifteen years old
Major interests: It used to be school; now I don't care. All I think about is how ugly I am.

"My aunt told me, 'When God handed out the looks in your family, you were behind the closet door.' I cried. She told me I shouldn't be so sensitive. She was just joking. Then she tried to make me feel better. 'The ugly duckling always turns into a swan.' I don't want to ever, ever talk to her again.

"You know what I feel like most of the time? Rotten. I have two sisters. They're very beautiful. I came out all wrong. Nothing went right. It's not fair. My dad tells me I can make people laugh and that's more important. A sense of humor is more important than having a pretty face. Who does he think he's kidding—me? Well, he's not the one called names in school and living with zits on his face.

"I try to tell my dad how I feel, and my mom, too. They won't listen. They don't have any idea how I feel. There are days when I try starving myself because I don't want to be fat and I don't want pimples all over my face.

"I don't like seeing myself in the mirror. I wish God made girls skinny and flat-chested. I get so depressed about having breasts. The boys all make fun of me when I go down the hall. I started wearing my older brother's jacket to school, but the teacher made me take it off. She said I couldn't wear the jacket in class. Oh God, how I burned inside. She had no idea how I felt. I do everything I can to hide my breasts, but they're obvious no matter what I wear. It's especially unfair to have sisters who are pretty.

"I would give anything in the world to have a pretty face and a body to match. I hate my sisters and I hate all pretty girls. I hate myself. Can't anyone understand why I feel this way? Wouldn't you, if you were me?"

Jason
Sixteen years old
Major interests: Working out; running; some school subjects.

Jason described himself as an average student who could, according to teachers and parents, do a lot better if he bothered applying himself. "I know my folks think I'm lazy. Dad tells me to get off my butt and do something like mow the lawn if I can't do my homework. Mom keeps talking about how when I was a little kid I was so terrific in school and at home because I helped out so much. I guess she remembers my taking out the garbage. Big deal.

"You know something? Listening to everybody is a 'pain in the butt!' I know what I look like. The pimples just came. I looked in the mirror one day and they were there. Mom took me to a doctor and I got some medicine, but I don't see it doing much good. That's why I want to keep my baseball hat on—to hide my face. You know what that got me? A call to the principal's office.

"Dad said I look like some damn 'hippie' with long hair. That, too, was done to cover my face. You see, no one understands why I do these things but me.

"I could take the pimples, I mean it, if I didn't look the way I do. I'm trying weights, but so far nothing works. I'm really working out, but still, nothing. I don't want to go into details, so just use your imagination. Girls don't go for guys like me; they run, and that hurts, you know. I'd like to ask this girl out, but I know the kind of guys her type goes for. Fat chance she would accept me. I'm the only guy among my friends who's got this problem. You must be kidding if you think I could just drop what's on my mind and study. I'm lucky to even be passing."

The tough answer:

How well we know your feelings. Jason and Francine, there isn't a teenager alive who, at one time or another, hasn't felt this very same way. Lots of people worry about their looks. That's normal. We all want to put our best foot forward. But there's a big difference between wanting to put our best foot forward and spending our lives in front of a mirror.

By all means, do what you can to make the most of yourselves. Just remember that during adolescence, the enormous changes that are occurring in your bodies pose different problems. First, there are hormones jumping around. Your muscle tone is changing, and there are all sorts of developmental transformations taking place. For example, right at this moment, Francine, you feel that your breasts are all out of proportion to the rest of your body. Jason, you haven't got the muscle tone you'd like to have. Each of you, like every other teenager, is in a growth spurt, developing and acquiring a body quite unlike the shape and form of your body in early childhood.

This doesn't mean for a moment that you should stop doing what you can while you wait until proportions catch up. Jason, work out to develop your body tone. Francine, you can choose clothes suited for your changing figure. Make sure you are taking care of your skin. You don't have to live with all the nuisances of adolescent physical problems.

But far more important are your egos in all of this. You know, some of the negative feelings you are experiencing are in your own minds. We once interviewed a beauty queen, and she was very unhappy because she had felt ugly since childhood. "Unbelievable," was our first reaction.

However, this was not the case. Sometimes we can convince ourselves that everything is a disaster when, in fact, it's not so terribly awful. We know that teenagers often engage in this kind of negative thinking. They may picture themselves as far worse than they are, building up horror stories in their minds about their appearance. They feel that no one loves them, that girls will run away from them and boys will flee, that their pimples are a nightmare and so forth—all because their bodies do not look like those they see in magazines or on TV.

Teenagers frequently get caught up in TV and Hollywood standards of beauty for themselves, all the while forgetting completely that much of what they see is the result of clever camera work and photo retouching. There's a big difference between reality and the image. *So don't let yourself be carried away with standards which, in reality, are based on some unreal false images and illusions.*

Be true to yourselves. Sure, do what you can about your appearance, but above all don't let the way you look control your life to the point that you lose sight of what really counts in life—the kind of person you are becoming and the lifetime values you are forming. And as for putdowns from other people—and we all have had verbal darts thrown our way at different times in our lives—there sure isn't a lot you can do. We're all for good interpersonal relationships, but, not everyone we meet is going to be kind or thoughtful. That's part of life. And during the teenage years, the attacks from peers and even misguided adults more often than not are directed toward the way one looks or dresses. Your response to all this is going to be "hear no evil, speak no evil, see no evil." Although the saying has been attributed to three monkeys, we think it's good advice for everyone.

The tough question:

"There are several things worrying me. What can I do about my fears and worries?"

"I'm afraid, afraid of growing up—college, grades, not getting a girlfriend, sex, drugs. You name it."

Craig
Sixteen years old
Major interests: None.

"I know people would laugh at me if they heard me saying this. I know my friends would crack up. That's not the way I come across to people. But right now it seems to me I'm just afraid of a helluva lot. I can't seem to get a hold on my feelings. They're all over the place. Like the other day I wanted so much to ask this girl out on a date. I knew she would accept. You know if someone is coming on to you. I acted like an idiot. She walked away and I don't blame her.

"My parents are hung up on me being so special. I have great friends, but I'd never tell them anything about my fears. It's just not the way guys talk. You keep this stuff to yourself. I don't even know if other guys feel like me.

"It's not all the time, but sometimes I feel as if I'm drowning in fear. It doesn't seem right. It's wrong, unnatural, and I get worried. I must be the only person in the whole world who gets scared like I get scared. Like coming home on a dark night, wondering if a gang is following me and if I'll get to the safety of my house. A guy like myself, almost seventeen, shouldn't be like this. It makes me feel as if I'm some kind of nerd. No one looking at me would ever guess what's in my head.

"I would give anything to talk to my parents, to someone, about being afraid; I mean, that's not life is it—fear? I've got to cope, don't I? I know that drugs are a real fear, sex is a real fear, but there must be some trick, some way to handle all this, or maybe I'm the only guy my age with this kind of problem." *(When Craig raised his concerns, he was absolutely convinced that he was the only guy in the world with this kind of worry. Far from it. What is particularly important for teenagers like yourself, Craig, is to realize that you're not alone. You know, sometimes, when things happen to us that get us down, frightened, we get the idea no one else has ever gone through the same experience. That's why we thought it would be interesting for you, Craig, to read what Mary Ann said about her life right now because both boys and girls in their teen years experience a lot of emotional ups and downs. After hearing from Mary Ann, we'll write our tough response.)*

"Inside my room everything is in its place. It's the world outside that gets me down, frightens me sometimes. I run scared, and that worries me."

Mary Ann
Seventeen years old
Major interests: Glee club; English; field hockey (I made the team!).

"It's not all of my life that bothers me. I think I'm luckier than a lot of kids. My mom and dad are great, and I don't have too many problems with my sisters. If you just look at my life and me from the outside, you'd think everything's perfect. It should be. But I'll tell you what's on my mind a lot—problems in the world I can't do anything about.

"My parents don't understand this. When I try and talk to them, I get the idea that my dad thinks I'm a silly and emotional girl. My mom, too, turns a deaf ear. But it's real, honest-to-God. If I see pictures in books or TV programs about nuclear war, I want to cover my head under a blanket.

"I'm scared of war, I'm scared of people getting killed and I'm scared of rape—you name it, I'm scared of it. It seems like problems are everywhere, and no one really cares about anyone but themselves. I feel so guilty about my life when I read or hear about kids my age who do not have anything—like homeless kids.

"I feel dumb talking about these things. Maybe you, too, will see me as an emotional teenager and make fun or say I'll grow out of this. Is it wrong for me to want to cry when I see photos of kids starving or kids killed in war or think of the madness that I read about in the newspapers day after day? Sure, it's not all the time that I feel like this, but so often I feel sad and guilty about everything I have.

"Only inside my room, everything is right. The bed-spread, curtains, the shelves with my Barbie doll collection from when I was a little kid. Of course, I don't play with them, but I keep them. My mom says someday I will have a daughter and want to pass them on, but I'm not so sure that I'm going to be around for this to happen.

"I never know when everything around me will start to crash. Everybody knows the world is a frightening place. I didn't think it was so dumb or strange when a couple of kids in my school committed suicide. I think I know how they felt. I don't even want to talk about it now because then I get to thinking about myself and how I feel inside, like I'm on a roller coaster at the top, and it's going fast, and there's only one way to go, and that is down."

The tough answer:

First of all, Craig and Mary Ann, we can't imagine dismissing your fears, worries, feelings of sadness or your unhappiness. We truly understand them. The blunt truth is there will always be times in your life when you're going to feel fearful, run scared, be less than happy or even unhappy. It would be great if life were all one smooth ride. But it's not. However, the things that frighten you inevitably will change as you grow older.

However, let's talk about the present. Moving from being a kid to a teenager can be a bit of a shock. One day you're carefree and feeling good, and the next day, or so it seems, your body begins playing tricks. Day by day you may be aware of changes in the way you feel.

However, when you are feeling low, it seems like those feelings are going to last forever, will never go away, no matter what you do. Anxiety and depression are fancy words for feeling lousy and not wanting to get out of bed in the morning, not wanting to do much of anything. These feelings can really throw one off balance. It's frightening to find yourself unhappy when, only a short time ago, you were a happy person. For example, there may be days when you don't want to do much of anything, not even go outside with your friends. Mary Ann, you mentioned fearing rape, nuclear war, the world's problems. Craig, you talked about fearing gangs and being afraid to ask a girl you like out on a date because she may refuse.

It's important for both of you to remember that these up-and-down troublesome concerns—fears, sadness, depression—are, more often than not, related to the great changes that are occurring in your hormones, your body chemistry. Up-and-down moods and extreme emotional reactions are part of growing up. In the developing process, normal biochemical changes take place, and these biochemical changes upset one's emotional balance. That's why sometimes you feel your emotions are on a roller coaster going from high to low and back up again. Just never forget that lows will be balanced by highs, and, more often than not, you'll find yourself in a pleasant middle ground.

Your body will adapt, and, as time goes on, you will find that your mood swings will lessen. However, as you grow into adulthood, it's a good time to try to take charge of yourself and your feelings. A three-year-old who doesn't get a much-wanted chocolate cookie throws a tantrum. The luxury of this kind of behavior isn't permitted a teenager.

Since this is the case, how can you take charge of yourself? One way is to deal with each fear or some otherwise negative state of mind *one at a time,* whether it is depression, anxiety or just plain feeling down. For example, Mary Ann, you have to be realistic. Rationally speaking, you must know that you can't solve the world's miseries. We don't want you to put blinders on, but the fact is, at this time in your life, you can't do much about the world's hunger. You can be a responsible person, but let's face it, you don't have the power to do much more. It would be great if you had the power to bring about large-scale changes and maybe someday you will be in a position to make a difference—to help stop a war or aid in stemming world hunger. But right now the reality is that you have a life to live and responsibilities to fulfill, so stick with what you can reasonably do at your age.

Let's take a second example of a fear you mentioned, Craig. There's nothing harder than asking someone out on a date for the first time and fearing a refusal. Did you ever think of coming out and being honest in such situations? How about telling the girl, "Look I don't want a refusal so I'm not sure about asking, so feel free to cut out before I try." If that girl is worth asking out, she will love the different approach. You've faced your worry.

Some fears make sense and we're sure you will recognize this fact. Fear of gangs, perhaps, where you live, Craig, is a real fear not to be discounted. You have to learn to position yourself apart. Mary Ann, concerns about attacks can be with good cause. Making sure you, too, aren't wandering around alone at times when there may be danger makes good sense. In other words, deal with each fear, remembering that the solving or coping with each specific fear is going to be different. ***Don't let fear rule you. You rule the fear by taking the right sort of action.***

The major point that we want to emphasize is that you can't run from your fears or from your ups and downs. They're real and, in a large part, stem from physical changes. Just for fun, we suggest that you chart your moods. Set up a calendar and note the mood of that day. And when a particular mood, for whatever unknown or known reason, makes you feel edgy, alone or scared, note that and take charge of yourself. That will be a day when you need your friends more than ever. You will need to go out and do something interesting with your pals. Along the same lines, telling someone how you feel will also help you more than you think. Telling your parents will be important. *Don't try to fight the low times alone. That's unwise. Just when you feel you should shut out the world and hide is exactly the time you must make yourself get out into the world.* The best cure for a wave of sadness is a special treat—a fun activity to get the roller coaster moving from a low point to a high one.

As for your parents thinking you're too emotional, too up and down, we don't really think this will be a problem. Granted, they may have forgotten their own teen ups and downs. However, *more than likely*, they just feel concerned because, when their kids have low periods, parents get uptight, too. They want to help, want to do whatever they can to smooth the way back to normalcy.

We've talked a lot about being strong because we want you to have faith in yourself. There are also times in everyone's life—whether rich and famous or not so rich and unknown—when we absolutely need another person to help us sort out our ups and downs. *Trust in one another is one of the important lessons to be learned as a teenager. Trust someone you care about—a friend, teacher, priest, parent or grandparent. Reach out for help if the "bumpy" time hangs in there too long. This is an absolute must.*

The tough question:

"Why can't I use contraceptives?"

"*If she gets pregnant, my girlfriend, I mean, then my life could be over. I don't know what to do. We love each other very much. This is the first girl I've ever wanted this way.*"

James
Seventeen years old
Major interests: My girlfriend; getting better grades; track team co-captain.

"My girlfriend and I have been going steady now for over six months. This is the first time I've had a serious relationship. My parents don't know and her parents don't know. They know we have dates, but they don't know how serious we are.

"We both want to have sex. It's not me forcing myself on her. She wants it as much as me. Neither of us wants sex just because we want to prove to the other kids we've had sex. We love each other very much.

"What's holding us back? Pregnancy. We try and tell each other that it couldn't happen, that we'd take precautions, but I'm not so sure. I mean, like all the time you hear about slips—accidents. There was a girl in our class last year who got pregnant—she was homecoming queen, no less. She dropped out of school. It kind of shook everybody up. Most of the kids think she had an abortion. One of the guys heard that her parents sent her away to have the baby. No one knows the real story for sure.

"We kind of worry because if it could happen to her, it could happen to us. The guy she was going with was a big shot in our school, captain of the football team. Both of us have old-fashioned parents. My mom and dad want me to go to college and they'd be pretty upset if they had any idea that I'm really committed to this girl, want to have sex and someday plan on the two of us getting married.

"What really bugs me is that my parents are two-faced. Since I was a little kid, my dad and my mom said, if I wanted to know something, I should ask them first because I could always trust my parents. Well, I did ask them about contraception. Well, what a switch. I tried to talk to my mom about condoms, and she nearly threw me out of the house for talking 'dirty' to her. I said, 'Mom, what's so dirty about condoms?' She threatened to tell my dad, but I don't dare go to him because he will just start giving me the big lecture about 'respect,' which has nothing to do with anything. Don't they have any idea of what it's like to be young and in love? Those two were **born** old.

"You know, when you're a kid you never think about your parents having sex. Yeah, other parents, but it's something you don't think about with your mom and dad. You don't even want the picture in your head. I want to ask them what they do. I mean they have three kids. Did they stop having sex because they didn't use contraception? Sean, my friend, has six brothers and one sister. OK, we know what must go on in his house, but I want to know the facts from my parents. I think it would be a lot healthier for me than to just find out in the locker room. What should I do for real protection? What should my girlfriend do? I figure they must know. Look at their lives.

"I owe a lot to my parents. I think I am a good person because of them. But then, when something really important comes up, like sex and contraception, they won't talk to me. I can't understand why. If I am supposed to go to them for help, for advice about everything, well why suddenly not contraception and sex? I don't like them turning me off because I want some honest answers. I need to know about contraception. I need to know what it is that makes everybody uptight about the subject. I have to make up my own mind, but an honest answer from people I respect would make me a lot happier."

> *"Does the church honestly believe that young Catholics like myself don't have sex before marriage? Why don't they accept that they do and learn to say that contraception is OK?"*
>
> *Carrie*
> *Sixteen years old*
> *Major interests: Good grades; partying; roller blading.*

"I don't get it. I really don't. The church saying, 'No way, contraception.' I mean, I don't even dare mention the word at home. I'm sure my mom has no idea that I know what I know. I haven't had sex and I'm not trying to play holier than thou. It's just that my boyfriend and I split up before we reached that decision. And you better believe me we were coming that close. I wonder what's going to happen with my next boyfriend?

"Of course, I was scared to go the whole way. I was scared about getting pregnant more than I was about sex. Actually, it's not fear of sex. I'm curious about what it feels like—not scared. I tried once talking to my mom and asking her what it felt like, and she got angry and walked away. I mean, talk about being open with your own mom. My friends who have had sex told me that it gets better when you do it more, but that still doesn't let me know what it feels like.

"I don't think parents, priests or teachers have any idea what goes on in kids' heads. I mean, here we are playing dumb about all this while everyone pretends it doesn't exist—sex, I mean; and it's everywhere. I guess it would be a lot easier on all of us if sex and having babies weren't tied up in a neat package. It's just not fair. In my mind, I don't see them all tied up. That's why I can't see what's so bad about contraception. I look at it this way. The church is against abortion—OK. I sort of go along with that. I mean it bothers me that a baby would be killed, and it absolutely doesn't matter if it's inside or outside the mother. Like I said, this makes sense. I know we should protect all life in our society. But contraception is a perfect way to prevent unwanted pregnancies. I mean, then there wouldn't be the problem of abortion. OK, so maybe there would be an accident, but really the chances are that pregnancy wouldn't happen. I just think it's time for a change. I think I have a right to know about contraception, and I have a right to use contraception. Don't you agree?"

The tough answer:

First of all, Carrie and James, we want you both to know that we really understand your frustration, annoyance and confusion about the whole business of sex—sexual behavior, contraception and sex outside of marriage. And we're going to deal with each of the issues you raised one by one. We are not going to hide behind our answers. That was a promise we made to you, and we've got to keep that promise.

Let's begin with the whole business of adults discussing sex with teenagers. We agree one hundred percent that it is rough having your parents preach to you about being open and honest, and then, when it comes to sex and you're open and honest, you get rewarded with anger. The plain truth is that parents, teachers, clergy and, for that matter, the vast majority of adults do have big problems talking about sexual desires, thoughts and behaviors with teenagers.

Just remember, most adults today probably grew up in a time when talk about sex, even mentioning the word *sex* or using the correct anatomical sexual terms—in fact anything to do with sexual activity—was taboo. It was more than a simple "no-no." We recall kids being thrown out of school for having the nerve to mention sex in front of a teacher. We're not talking about having sex. We're talking about *talking* about sex. One man recalls having his mouth washed out with laundry soap by a furious parent because he blurted out sexual words.

It's a different world out there now—a different ball game. That is troublesome for adults who are playing by the old rules. They have a tough time giving up their inhibitions and tolerating knowledge about sex in teenagers, whom they think are still too young to handle such things. It's unfortunate, but try to be understanding with your mom and dad. If talking about sex makes them feel uncomfortable, just remember it's not easy for them to change old habits of thinking and behaving. It's not a matter of right or wrong—it's just a fact of life. We bet your parents could discuss sex with someone else's kid—it's just that with one's own kid, such discussions make one feel "hot under the collar." A parent simply doesn't like the thought of one's own child having sex, just as kids feel uneasy thinking that their parents have sex. OK for everyone else, but not in the family. That is precisely why outside resources, like this book, are best for a lot of kids when it comes to sexual guidance.

Now let's move on a bit. For most of you, up until the teen years life went along pretty smoothly. Suddenly in adolescence all the hormones kick in. Sexual urges, sexual drives come into play. It's hard. It really is. We'd like to tell you that sexual urges will calm down. We'd like to be able to tell you that they can be repressed. We can't. That's just *not* the way life is. The reality is that for the rest of your life, beginning with the teen years, at different times sexual urges, desires and thoughts are going to be part of your life. There are times, of course, when they will be less powerful than at other times. There are also going to be plenty of occasions when the desires will be overwhelming and almost impossible to bear. Now, given this bit of reality, with a whole lifetime ahead of you, learning something about controlling your sexual urges, putting them on hold until marriage, isn't the worst thing in the world, is it?

Sure, you would like everything right now. You don't want to wait. After all, you waited for a driver's license until you were old enough. You have to wait a while until you're old enough to vote. A lot of privileges in life are age related. That's unfair, you say. But doesn't this make sense? Doesn't a kid have to wait until he or she is old enough before crossing a busy street? Would you let a six-year-old do this? No, of course not. That's absurd. So, you see, age-related controls just filter through a lot of things in life—not just sex.

What do we mean by "old enough" with respect to sex? Yes, you are old enough for the sexual act now, perhaps, but are you old enough to handle marriage? Do you want to get married now? Do you want that kind of responsibility? OK, you say, you don't want to get married but sex can occur outside of marriage. *Of course it can.* We don't deny that in the least. You say, doesn't the church know that this happens? It's not a matter of whether the church knows something or your parents know something. It's a matter of whether the behavior is grounded in morality. Of course, the clergy and most adults are fully aware that sexual activity goes on among teenagers. You'd be surprised to know how much they really know. The fact that sexual activity *does* go on doesn't mean that this is the kind of behavior that is appropriate for the age or for the spiritual values of the people involved.

Yes, of course, contraception could prevent unwanted pregnancies. And, it is a fact that the question of contraception *within marriage* has been under a lot of discussion. The official position of the church is absolutely clear with regard to this matter, and a number of Catholic theologians have been arguing that church doctrine should be changed. *When* or *if* such a change will occur, we certainly cannot predict. Who knows what the doctrines will be fifty or one hundred years from now? Also, when you bring up the point that contraception must have occurred in your family, it is neither of interest nor concern to us. You may be right or wrong. That's not the issue, because the use or methods of prevention *within a marriage are not* within the scope of this book. But both liberal and conservative theologians as well as your parents and other adults would argue that no contraception should be used *outside of marriage* because there shouldn't be any sex outside of marriage in the first place.

If contraception is permitted in any form, then sexual activity would be encouraged. *And the church position about sexual relations outside of marriage is absolutely straightforward—everyone agrees—absolutely not.*

Is the church being old-fashioned? Are these rules that label sex outside of marriage as sinful now archaic? We know teenagers are asking these kinds of questions. "Hey, we're modern. Those are old-fashioned ideas. The church should 'get with it.'" Yes, we suppose in a way that the church does have some rules or ideas that *appear* old-fashioned because they have been around a long time. But, in a significant way, some of these so-called old ideas are really new ideas. We say this without one bit of hesitation. In the modern rush of the world today despite even the fanciest of computers and the biggest of scientific breakthroughs, *love and a meaningful relationship between two people is still the number one dream and ambition for everyone.* It's been that way since the beginning of time and will undoubtedly last a lot longer than any of us. If that's what *old-fashioned* means, then so be it.

You kids will agree with us when we say that the one-on-one bond between two people is more important than anything else. And the one-on-one bond that culminates in a sexual act of love and procreation is truly special. Just don't forget that no one—not the church, your teachers, adults or parents—is saying no to sex forever. All they hope is that you hold off until the time is right for the natural, God-given purpose of sex to unfold, and that is *within the institution of marriage.* Then and only then, love and having kids will follow a natural course.

Pregnancy, as you yourself said, James, is a real possibility. There is no guarantee that it won't happen. And that's something you don't want and neither does your girlfriend. You're risking everything, aren't you—sort of playing Russian roulette? All the tensions, all the fears that you have about the possibilities of pregnancy are real.

It won't be easy holding off. We recognize this. But you know something? A little wait can make the reward even sweeter. The time will come when marriage and sex will follow naturally. Not only will it be more enjoyable for the two of you, but you will feel a sense of worth and dignity, and, in a world where so many values have been tossed in the garbage, this can mean something.

We suggest that, rather than look at church doctrines as heavy-handed rules curbing all your fun and games, maybe you should turn all this around and ask yourself some questions like, "If I play fun and games outside of marriage, do I run the risk, not only of committing a sinful act, but of tarnishing something that is going to be a very special part of my life with my wife or husband for the rest of my life?" This, you have to agree, is something worth thinking about.

The tough question:

"What can I do about trying to live up to the unrealistic expectations that my parents have?"

"My folks want a winner. They got me for a son. I'm not a loser, but no way can I live up to their dreams. My parents want so much from me. What can I do?"

Kevin
Seventeen years old
Major interests: Math; sports.

Kevin, two younger sisters and their parents live in a single-family suburban home large enough for each youngster to have a private room. Although both parents work full-time, they are in close contact with their children, supportive of their activities and respectful of their private lives.

"They're good to me. They're great. My dad and I spend time together, and he always comes up with money when I need it, and my mom and I get along just fine. That's the problem. If I had parents like some of my friends, then I'd have a legitimate gripe. It's hard to put into words. It's not that they do anything bad. *Honest to God I wish they did.* I wish my mom would scream or something. I wish my dad would cut off my allowance, ground me, keep me from using the car—anything. So what gives? I'll tell you what gives. I'm not what they want. I know it. They just won't accept it. *I'm not the best because I just can't live up to their dreams.*

"My dad sees me as number one. I bring home a B, and I tell you the world drops out from under him. I know it. He doesn't come out and say anything real mean. He doesn't have to because I can read it in his face. I know what he's thinking. Maybe he'll say, 'Almost there, Kevin,' in this off voice. They've got so much invested in me as a person that I feel like my back is being broken. I know deep down there's a good reason. My dad never went to college. He's told me not once but a thousand times that he wishes he could have had the advantages I have. He doesn't make me feel guilty or anything like that; he just says, it's great, that I don't really have to work, and can spend time on school work. He had to work when he was my age while he went to high school.

"He's got great hopes for me. The problem is that I'm not all that great. Deep down I know it. He won't believe it, but it's there all right. In my mom and dad's heads, they feel that 'Kevin should be top of the class or Kevin should have won the trophy.'

"I'm not as smart as they think I am. There are a lot of kids a helluva lot smarter than me, better looking, better athletes. I know the score. I know what I am. I tell you, being second rate is killing me. I would like to be myself. I would like to do what I can the best way I know how, but my best is not their best. It's never going to be their best because of their own dreams.

"My mom talks about me going to some good college. She says that's why she's working and saving money—to pay tuition. I'm scared that I'm not going to get in *any* college. I keep pushing myself. You know, sometimes I sit with a book in front of me before a test and I just keep staring at the page. You know what? Half the time I haven't read a word or seen anything. All I think about is what mom and dad expect from me.

"I try telling my dad, 'I'm not tops in the class. I'm not all that great,' and every time, he says to me, 'Kevin, you are number one—just work a little harder.' I feel sick to my stomach when he says that. He really believes what he says. I don't understand him. I think he must be nuts or something, believing and saying 'Kevin, you're number one.'

"I'm not all that bad. I'm just an ordinary guy, maybe a little smarter than some, but I'm not going to set the world on fire. I wish I could make my parents believe I'm not trying to hurt them. I'm not trying to ruin their lives. I'm only worried that I'm going to disappoint them because I'm not going to be that first-place winner they've got pictured in their minds.

"That kind of scares me. Sometimes I lie to make them happy. OK. That's what happened. I feel guilty. I told my parents I had the best grade on a major test in history. My mom was so happy. That's what killed me inside. She told my dad. I tried to tell myself it wasn't a big lie. I could have meant a lot of different things by "best" grade. Maybe it was *my* best grade. I'm kind of lying now. I don't want to lie ever again like this. I don't want to pretend anymore to them or to myself. It's tough luck that my folks got me for a son. My folks want a winner, but they got me. I'm not a loser. But there's no way that I can live up to their dreams."

The tough answer:

Number one, the hotshot son, the son who is a winner— you find this all hard to believe, Kevin, that your mom and dad could see you this way. It's not a question of right or wrong or whether it's good or bad, but the blunt, inescapable truth is that *a lot of parents need to see their kids this way.* And, what's more, they really believe it's so. In many parents' eyes, their child is always super, the best ball player, the best swimmer, the best in lots of things.

Let's turn all of this around. How would you feel if your parents kept calling you a loser, a failure? Chances are, you wouldn't be all that happy. We happen to think you're *lucky* that your parents feel good about you. In fact, one of the big mysteries of the life of a parent is the belief that one's child is *special.* Now it is also a fact that parents are human. They can make mistakes. They have faults. They can *overdo* this special line. They can easily lose sight of reality.

We aren't out to criticize your parents. We appreciate their need to see you as special. We appreciate their dreams about you and their hopes for you. But it may be true they are driving home the message with just a bit too much force.

The record has to be set straight for them. We think that all parents can benefit from a few suggestions about child rearing. And, contrary to what you may think right now, parents can be open to suggestions. Of course, a lot is going to depend on the way you or anyone else for that matter, goes about correcting or judging what they do or say.

There's no point in attacking. You're going to be sensible and rational, and we bet you they will react the same way.

However, before we go on to make a few suggestions, we want to be sure that you are being **totally honest** with yourself. Are you using your parents' behavior as an *excuse* for not performing to the best of your abilities? Are you putting the blame on your parents? We're going to take what you said at face value. We're going to assume that you aren't kidding yourself and that you are trying your best. We're going to believe you when you say that your parents are the ones overdoing the pep talks about trying harder and doing better.

If you really *are* knocking yourself out, working hard, not goofing off, and are still falling short of your parents' expectations, we agree that this is a tough position. No doubt about it. Just keep in mind that this happens to many people. Some parents try to live out their lives in their children. These parents may try to get their kids to achieve what they didn't accomplish in life, or there may be other problems in the family that they hope their kids' success will compensate for.

Clare's parents, for example, are depending upon her to be a high achiever because she has a kid brother who is in special classes. Every grade of hers counts in their eyes because they want her to be a star performer. She, too, doesn't feel all that outstanding and she is driving herself as if she were in a constant race, trying to run faster, jump higher and get better grades than anybody. Instead of achieving a stellar performance, she's miserable and tense because deep down she doesn't feel all that great. She feels driven only because she knows how much her accomplishments mean to her parents. Clare told us, "I feel like a fake inside. I can't be the best in school. I'm not all that super, and I'm the first one to admit it to myself. I'm no hotshot, and I am tired of all this lying to myself and to everybody else. I want to stop lying and just be myself."

There's no question that parental pressure is rough for you, for Clare and for lots of others.

Now let's talk about what ideas we have about handling parental pressures like this. Though we're responding to you, Kevin, these same suggestions will be helpful to Clare and anybody else facing the same kind of problem. First of all, you are going to stop lying to parents about grades or about anything else. It isn't worth it in the long run. Lying "small" soon turns into lying "big"; plus, they'll find out that you're lying sooner or later. You've heard the old saying that "everything comes out in the wash." When this happens, you'll be the one ending up feeling guilty, and that's definitely not how you should feel. You are *not* guilty. If, indeed, you *are trying your best*, your conscience is clear, so there's no reason in the world that you have to lie or try to fool anybody. What you must do is try to be consistently straight with your parents.

Let's take grades. You show your dad your grades and his face falls. You read the sadness in his expression. Without defenses, without kidding around, let him know in plain talk, "Look, Dad, I did what I could do. I studied. These grades don't make me happy either. But that's the way it is. What I will tell you and what I can promise is that I'll keep plugging away and do the best I can. That's fair, isn't it? I'm not a super star. I can try, though, to do a lot better, and I will give it my best shot."

Of course, you will want to say this in your own words, but what we want to make sure is that from now on you're going to be totally frank and aboveboard with your parents about what is happening in school. No more lying, no more hiding. And, when you stop hiding and lying, you're going to feel great because you won't have all those guilty feelings about yourself and your performance. Feeling guilty is a sure way to make you feel tense.

We don't want to fault your mom. We wonder if she may not realize that she is making you feel guilty because she is working hard to earn money for your college expenses. The plain truth is that she really is trying to earn money for just that reason. However, knowing that she is doing this certainly doesn't make you happy either.

We suggest that you tell her flat out that you wish she wouldn't make this kind of sacrifice. You appreciate her help and you're going to try hard to do your best, but it doesn't make you feel good knowing that she is knocking herself out at her job and thinks that you're goofing off at school and not appreciating her hard work. None of this is quite the case, of course. Tell her you'll do your best; she can help, but you don't want her giving up so much for you. Level with your dad and level with your mom without anger, without defensiveness. This is not a time for a shouting match. You are going to be the one in control, helping them see things from your point of view.

Changing the way you look at the situation will relieve you of a lot of stress. We suspect you're feeling a lot of tension, which isn't going to do you much good when test-taking time comes around. And, as far as your dad's beliefs about you are concerned, he thinks that his son, is a very special person—well, that's not exactly the worst thing in the world, is it? *You are special in his eyes—so be it. In a way, it's kind of great, isn't it, knowing your dad backs you all the way with his faith and concern?*

The tough question:

"What do I do about the 'crazy' thoughts I have sometimes?"

"I'm worried. I wonder if there's something abnormal about me. I think dirty thoughts. Sometimes I watch late-night porno films on TV. I can't stop myself."

Billy
Sixteen years old
Major interests: Soccer; getting a girlfriend; better grades, to make my parents happy.

"If you just look at me from the outside," said Billy, "you'd see a different person from the 'me' inside. I'm not the same. This drives me crazy—knowing that I've got a habit of thinking 'dirty thoughts.' It happens to me enough to make me wonder if I'm okay. I don't know if it happens to other people. I don't have anyone to ask. I'm going along like everything's fine—playing soccer, going to class—and then it comes on me like a bolt, and I can't stop myself. The dirty thoughts I mean, like seeing girls and thinking what I think.

"I sneak looks at porno movies, and I've begun to hate myself. I've gotten up at night and turned on the TV. The rest of my family are asleep, I'm all alone in front of the TV, hating myself for what I'm doing. I want to stop. I'm scared of what will happen to me if I keep on like this.

"My parents don't have any idea what is going on, like what is happening. I think it would kill my mom. She's got this idea that I'm a good kid. Like she tells people she doesn't have problems with me—drugs, smoking and things like that. I worry my dad would beat the heck out of me. My parents are super straight. They don't drink or swear or anything like that.

"I'd never talk about this with my friends. I'm telling this to you only because you don't really know me, my friends or my family. You don't know where I live, my address or anything. You just know my first name, and maybe that's not even my name.

"The other guys joke a lot, you know, dirty jokes, but it's all out in the open, and that is why I feel what I do in secret is wrong. That bothers me. I'm the guy who doesn't tell dirty jokes, and yet I know I'm the rotten one in the bunch.

"It's like an obsession that I can't stop. I try to stop, but then it seems as if I do it even more. I'm too ashamed to say what the thoughts are, but, if you think the worst, the dirtiest thoughts you can imagine, then you'd know for sure what goes on in my head.

"All I'd like is for someone to tell me what I can do to stop, and if there's anything abnormal about me. I'd give anything just to be a normal kid. That's what I'm worried about more than anything—being some weird, 'sicko' kind of guy."

The tough answer:

Billy, let's set the record straight for you and for lots of other kids who will be reading about the topic you brought up. We were going to use the word *problem,* but that's all wrong because what's happening to you is *not* a problem. By this we mean that you're not weird; you're not sick; you're not any of those things. We are going to tell you flat out that there isn't anyone, and we mean *anyone* who hasn't, at some time or another, shared your experience of thinking those things that you call "dirty" thoughts. And this is a fact. Saints and sinners alike have all had thoughts they would rather not admit to.

We'd like to start out by dropping the word "dirty." We think it will be better for you if we just call them **thoughts you'd rather not have,** and, in this sense, we agree with you. The thoughts are wasting your time, making you feel guilty and uncomfortable. Naturally, life would be more pleasant and comfortable if you didn't have these thoughts.

First of all, we do think the idea of your getting up at night and turning on the TV is a good place to start dealing with the issue. If you turn on the TV, try another program. You may go back to the porno stuff, but give yourself a chance to look at something else. You can also take this approach at other times when an obsessive thought or idea comes into your mind; you just can switch the "channels" in your head and think other thoughts until the obsession eventually disappears. You may even become bored and tired of the same thoughts.

Above all, don't be scared. You're only making things worse for yourself by feeling scared or telling yourself you're scared. Accept the tendency to think about things you'd rather *not* think about as just a *phase of life.* As your interests broaden and you get involved in other activities, you will be surprised to find that unwelcome thoughts decrease and fade away naturally. It will also help if you remember that you're not a saint; you're not an angel; you're human.

We don't want you to feel ashamed; we don't want you to feel guilty. The fact that you were able to bring this topic up tells us something. You're a lot stronger than you give yourself credit for. We think that you or any teen going through this obsessive kind of stage in your thinking should realize that, *over time*, the intensity will dwindle.

Your task is to let these ideas run their course in your mind. Make new opportunities for yourself, watch other programs, get out with your friends and, if you can, share these thoughts. You're going to be surprised to find out that other teens, too, have gone through or are going through similar experiences.

We assure you, the day will come when you're worn out from a rough soccer game, have asked that girl you've admired in your class out on a date, and have a grade jumped a whole letter, that you will flick on the TV and see the porno films for what they are—boring, silly, tiresome kinds of shows not worth your time or effort. A brief titillation, and you have moved on with your life.

The tough question:

"I think there are some things really wrong with the church. What should I do about this?"

"I can't say one word of criticism about the church, or my mother explodes."

Nancy
Seventeen years old
Major interests: Math; science; field hockey; anything related to business and finance—I seem headed in that direction.

"My whole family are good Catholics, and I don't mean just going to mass and that, but really trying to live by the principles of our faith. My aunt and uncle are different. They call themselves 'cafeteria Catholics.' My uncle says that he believes some things and makes up his own mind on other things. I don't know exactly what they believe and what they don't because they don't tell me, of course. I suspect that I know one thing. My aunt had an abortion. She has four kids, and I heard her tell my mom that she was pregnant and that she didn't want the fifth kid. It was all secret. I didn't see her for a while. Then, the next time I saw her she wasn't pregnant. My mom was crying; my grandma, too. It was a mess. I wasn't supposed to know, obviously.

"Anyhow, I think our family is different because we live next door to my grandparents, and they are the kind—my grandmother mostly—who could go to mass a dozen times a day and it wouldn't be enough. My mom is influenced by my grandmother. I don't have any doubts about this.

"When I was small, I never questioned anything about the church. What I was taught, I believed, and I didn't misbehave. I don't have plans to misbehave now, but Mom acts like this is what is going to happen. She keeps asking me whether or not I have done anything with boys. She can't even bring herself to say the word 'sex.' She's always telling me boys aren't to touch me. I got her really mad when I asked 'where exactly they weren't supposed to touch me.' She really explodes if I try to talk about abortion or contraception. She acts like if I even think about these things I'll go to hell. This bothers me. She's so sane about everything else but when it comes to the church and her beliefs, she becomes rigid.

"Why can't she talk to me? Why can't I question the church? Sure, I can go to our priest and get answers, but I would like some answers from her that clarify what she feels and what she believes. Does she really agree with everything the church says or does?

"I can't say the same for myself. I am bothered by different things. Like last Sunday, there was another sign at the collection basket for the archbishop's annual appeal. There always seems to be a lot of appeals and a lot of asking for money. It's not only money, of course, but rules about sex, contraception and dating. I mean, this is the twentieth century. It's not medieval times. Maybe it was different way back when.

Now what really bugs me the most is the church's attitude toward women. Why can't women become priests? It's not that I want to become a priest, but I do not like the idea of being a second-class citizen. It's all wrong. I think it's wrong that priests can't marry. Why can't they marry? Why can't they have children? The church is in the dark ages. I am not alone in thinking all of this. I have girlfriends who say they are going to stop going to church until there are women priests in existence. I know guys who say they would think about being priests only if priests could marry.

It's crazy. I mean this is practically the twenty-first century, and the old men in the church act like it was the same as way back in the old days. Don't they know what is going on? Don't they have any idea that people might do something like my uncle and aunt did and then hide this from the priests? I don't want to hide. I would rather be up front and find out how my mom feels and get some straight answers. I am not sure how I'll feel about the answers, but I need something other than just this old, blind acceptance of my mom and my dad, too. My grandmother is different. I understand why she can't change at her age. She's pretty old.

"What really gets to me is not being able to question the church, as if I were some sort of dummy. I mean that's just not fair. Everywhere in school they keep saying that students should ask questions. Then, bingo, when it comes to the church, the door shuts—no more questions allowed. I'd like to know from someone why my questioning is wrong?"

The tough answer:

The question you raise, Nancy, is one that we feel is extremely important to answer. Nothing can be more frustrating in life than to have questions, reasonable questions, and have everyone "run" from giving open and honest answers. It *does* concern us that your mother evades *all* questions; however, we *do* understand her position and would like to offer an explanation for her behavior. She may feel that if you question too much, you may retreat from religion, lose your faith and you may stop believing, and that worries her. However, we would like you and her to understand that we feel somewhat differently about this matter.

It is our opinion that intelligent questions won't undermine a faith but, rather, will enhance it. Let us explore this with you. *By raising the issues you have posed, we feel that you and other teenagers are not challenging the fundamental teachings of Christ. The church's belief system is not what is troubling you. What is troubling, what is disturbing are the interpretations and applications of these teachings or principles to specific, current and concrete issues.*

Now this can sound pretty elitist, but let's give an example. The position of the church is that Catholic couples should practice responsible parenthood, but artificial contraception is always wrong. However, the use of the sterile period through the rhythm method, or natural family planning, is morally acceptable. And, within the Catholic Church, not all agree with this official teaching. Over time, however, this notion has become policy. And it might surprise you to know that responsible theologians as well as ordinary people continue to be engaged in lively debate on the subject. In other words, this very sensitive issue is being discussed and questioned by people from all walks of life.

There is nothing wrong, we believe, with questioning on any and all levels. In fact, questioning should be encouraged, *if the goal of the questioning is greater understanding.* Trying to find out more, learn more, improve one's thinking and enhance one's understanding is extremely valuable. Blind faith serves no good purpose. *Faith with understanding can lead to true belief.*

The problem is that sometimes questioning is just done as a way of rebelling against authority, just because authority is authority. It's a matter of "I'll show them I can be my own person." Such behavior serves no purpose.

Let's take the issue of priests marrying or why women can't be priests. We quite understand your feelings about being a second-class citizen. Why shouldn't you be able to celebrate the Eucharist or hear confessions? And for guys like Steven, who have thought about becoming priests and resent not being able to marry, this same sort of questioning of authority can arise. It is not within the scope of this book to answer all of these *specific* questions, but we definitely support your right to inquire *why.* For example, you have a right to know why the church's position is that men and women can have separate and yet equal roles, but that women are becoming increasingly active in church affairs.

Steven, too, can ask his question and find out exactly why celibacy for priests came into being and why some individuals today are arguing for a change in canon law.

Questioning as a step toward learning is important. *However, there is also a time to listen to those with experience.*

You should know that you kids are not the first to come up with these kinds of questions: Should priests marry? What about abortion and contraception? Should nuns be allowed to marry? If a woman is pregnant out of wedlock can a priest allow her to be married in the church? Can gays get married in the church? Why are gays condemned by the church? What's so horrible about masturbation? These are just a few of the many, many questions you kids have handed us. We unequivocally support your right to ask these questions of responsible authorities, whether they be priests, nuns, teachers or other adults.

However, we would like to note that some of these problems are complex. And to deal with the answers rationally and morally requires a lot of experience and knowledge. *You have to pay attention to the views of people who have this knowledge and have devoted time to these issues.*

Some of the answers may be based on just plain history, that is, historical precedent. This is the way it has been for centuries, and so be it. This won't make some of us happy, will it? But then, just to change with the wind or on a whim can also be dangerous. *There is sometimes a value in consistent, traditional behavior. Knowing that something has been done one way for centuries gives us a bond with the past and a tie-in with the future.*

We'd also like to add that change just for change's sake has its good and bad points. For example, change is sometimes stimulating. Nancy, just as an example, let's say you've worn your hair long and suddenly decide to cut it short. Or you, Steven, decide an earring in your ear and long hair will suit you just fine. You both do these things and find yourselves enjoying being the objects of interest and attention from your friends. However, after a while, the new styles may bore you, and you shift back or do something else. In life, we're always making changes to keep from getting bored or just to spark up our lives. You know, one year platform sneakers are in, and the next they're out. One year patched jeans are the rage; the next, you had better have jeans without holes if you want to look cool. You may plaster your bedroom walls with posters of favorite rock stars or decide you want a polka dot ceiling and striped walls. Great—you have your fun and grow out of these things.

However, change regarding long-term traditions and morality issues is another story. We're not talking about striped walls or earrings in one ear. These changes hit at the core of the human spirit and sense of morality, and demand more thought before a change is made. Yes, the church is slow to change. You're not the only ones who want faster changes, but a change about the basic moral issues of life is not quite the same as orange stripes on a bedroom wall or new rock posters. Think about this. Rock stars go out of fashion. The orange stripes drive you crazy. So you shift to something else.

The reality here, however, is that the church is more than one individual, and any changes it makes cannot be equated with a decision about orange stripes. Changes in the church necessarily have to take place more slowly. *However, the basic notion you both have about the need and importance of change is by no means wrong. It's just the direction and the speed that have to be taken into account.*

Nancy, you will have to go easy on your mom at this point. We think that if she understands you aren't challenging her or rebelling against the moral beliefs and underlying code of your faith, she may respond quite differently. You're not giving up on your faith. You want to know more so that what you do, how you behave, is more meaningful. Question, by all means; *don't waste your effort in rebellion for rebellion's sake.* See if the answers you get make sense and fit what you know to be a decent moral code.

We all have to recognize our own limitations about some of these matters. However, just because we don't know something, doesn't mean we shouldn't ask. We also have an obligation to listen and to take advantage of the knowledge and experience of others. Just remember, there are going to be people who resist being questioned, and who are reluctant to change. *But you're also going to find that there are plenty of others who realize that questioning, analyzing and thinking, strengthen the mind of a true believer. And these same people will foster appropriate changes.*

"How can I deal with the death of someone close to me?"

"*There was something I was going to tell Mom before she died. I can't remember what it was. When do I stop missing her?*"

Beth
Fifteen years old
Major interests: Piano; reading; mostly thinking about boys in my free time.

Beth lives with her father and two younger brothers. Several days a week a part-time housekeeper visits the home; however, Beth's father hopes an elderly aunt will move in with the family on a full-time basis.

"My dad says we need someone," said Beth. "I told him that my brothers and I can manage. It's only been a couple of months since Mom died. Besides, I don't need anyone around to take Mom's place. She was dying, for a year before—cancer. Everybody in the family expected her to die. That was true. It was like everyone was waiting around for it to happen, wondering why it was taking so long. I even heard my aunt talking. She didn't think I heard what she said, 'When do you think she'll die?' and 'How much longer can she hang in there?'

I don't have anyone I can ask about Mom, like what really happens to her when the casket goes into the ground. That sounds stupid, doesn't it? That's not what I mean. It's such an end, like forever, if you know what I mean. I got so that I stopped thinking about her a lot when she was still alive. I had to because it hurt so much, because she was so sick. Then she died, and it's been terrible for me.

"I feel so guilty, like when I hung out at the mall with my friends and, you know, talking about boys, and she was dying. Now I think about her all the time. I seem to remember everything she said to me. I remember her blowing her top at me once, pulling my hair, and me fighting her, and we both said terrible things, and she sent me to my room. I told her I wasn't going to go. We stood in the kitchen, the two of us glaring at each other. It was because I told her I liked this guy, and no matter what she said, I was going to go out with him. It seems so stupid and petty now, thinking back. Why do I keep remembering bad things?

"I loved her so. I loved my mom. I can't stop thinking about the awful things, though. I can't think of the good things. It's like there never was anything good. It was all bad. My dad asked me to tell him what I remember best about mom, and I said 'nothing.' That wasn't true. I just said that. He told me it was a terrible thing to say. I guess it was, and I'm sorry, but I can't tell my dad or my brothers.

"It's just the four of us now in the house. My dad is tired a lot from work. He gets home late. My brothers have been real good, maybe better than me. I've been the bad one. Sometimes, when I'm reading a book, I stop, and I see my mom in the doorway. I can see her like she was really there.

"At night, before I go to sleep is when I think the most. I try to remember what it was I wanted to tell her. I can't remember; it bothers me a lot. Dad says Mom wouldn't want me to stop my life now just because she's dead. He says we all have to build our lives again because this is what Mom would want. Dad's lying to me. Everybody's lying to me. How does he know what she wanted? She wasn't even talking much those last months. I don't even want to tell you how she looked when we went to visit her in the hospital. We had to do that. Dad said it was better for her and for all of us.

"I wish someone would tell me how long I'll feel like this. When does it start getting better? When do I forget she died? When do I stop seeing her in the doorway of my room just before I turn out the light to go to sleep? There was something I was going to tell Mom before she died. I wish I could remember what it was."

"I know everyone is going to die someday. I don't want to think about it. I don't want to talk about it. I'm scared."

Michael
Sixteen years old
Major interests: Baseball; biology.

Michael lives with his parents on the second floor of a two-family residence. His grandparents have the first-floor apartment. From an early age, Michael has moved freely between both apartments. "If my parents weren't home, I went to Grandma's house. After my mom went back to work, I went there every day after school."

"My grandfather and I spent a lot of time playing. When he was young, he wanted to be a ball player, but it never worked out that way. He was like the guy in the movie, you know, *Field of Dreams*. When I started playing ball in high school, he was there at every game yelling his head off. The day I got my school letter he gave me money for a sweater. He's a great guy, and that's what my problem is all about.

"When I was small, I just thought he would live forever. Kids don't think about death. Yeah, you play with toy guns and kill people and stuff like that, but "you're dead" doesn't have any real meaning. I once had a dog that died, and I felt so bad. But my folks got another dog a week later, so I wasn't all that upset for very long.

"This past year has made me think differently about everything. My grandfather had a small stroke. I wasn't at home when it happened. I was at school. I found out he was taken to the hospital. I knew that any day it could happen—my grandfather dying.

"Luckily, he pulled out of the stroke. But now his mouth is all crooked. One side of his face is twisted. I don't notice it anymore, but other people do. He doesn't speak clearly.

I understand him, I really do, even though he sometimes has to repeat himself a couple of times before I catch on to what he's trying to say. He walks stiffly and that's because of the stroke. One side never got better.

"It bothers me a lot to think about how he is and it's even worse when people talk. My grandmother will say, 'When Grandpa dies, I'm packing my suitcase and moving into a home. Your parents can have the whole house.'

"I tell her not to talk like that. Maybe Grandpa is not really as deaf as she thinks. It's hard to get her to stop. I find myself lately thinking a lot about death, and I think about my parents—that the same thing could happen to them. I have a friend whose mom died. He started acting strange after that. He didn't want to hang out with the rest of us. I don't think her dying meant much to any of us, but it's a lot different when it happens in your own family.

"I know that everyone has to die and I know it's part of life. But what doesn't make sense to me is why people have to keep talking about it. Why can't they keep these thoughts to themselves? It bothers me that my parents don't seem to understand how I feel. The other day at dinner my mom said, 'Grandpa could go anytime.' She meant *die*, of course. She was worried about him dying in the house and upsetting everyone.

"It sounded bad, but I know she's really sad and depressed about how sick he is. I couldn't stand listening to them, so I got up and went to my room. I lay down on the bed, not crying or anything, I just stared at the ceiling. There was a spot up there where I had tossed a baseball. I kept looking at the spot and I felt scared, real scared."

The tough answer:

"How right you are, Michael, when you said that little kids playing games, falling down dead or whatever, haven't any idea of the real meaning behind their actions. You and Beth are confronting death—in your case, Michael, the possibility of the death of a loved grandfather, and, you, Beth, the death of your mom. As one gets older, the reality of death and the possibility of death become *much* too real for comfort.

Being scared of death is normal. Most people are. They don't even want to think about it. Sometimes they may go to great lengths not to even say the word. They talk about going to heaven or the "great beyond." Death can sometimes make the living uncomfortable.

There are also others who make themselves face the possibility of death. They confront death head-on. We think, Michael, that this is what your grandmother may be doing—trying to handle the possibility of her husband dying by planning for the future. It may also be why your mother talks about her dad "going" anytime now.

The point is that people do different things to help them handle their feelings. Your grandmother and your mother have chosen ways that make you uncomfortable. You would rather repress, avoid the topic, not think about it because you get tight inside and upset or scared. *There really isn't a best way for everybody.* Some individuals have to talk about death, and others may want to shut death out of their thinking. You have to decide what's best for you. We just don't want you to think of your grandmother or your mother as unfeeling people. They just have to behave in ways that make them comfortable.

We think that what might also be bothering you, Michael,

and certainly what disturbs you, Beth, are concerns about loss. Beth, you've lost a mother. Michael, you feel threatened because you know deep down your grandfather is on shaky ground and may die any time now. How do you handle all this?

Beth, you've handled it all by being angry at your mom. This is very common—getting angry at the person who dies. That person had no business dying. Didn't that person have any idea how those who lived on might feel? This is all quite irrational. It isn't as if the person made a conscious choice to die just to be hurtful. That's what made you angry, Beth, and so you are thinking about bad things that she did so you won't feel guilty or responsible for her death.

Michael, you're thinking ahead to the time when your grandfather may die, preparing yourself for the inevitable. But, if and when he does die, you too may feel anger and hurt because he left you behind when he knew how important he was in your life.

There is a very special sort of anger. It's an anger based on love, sadness and regret. The anger will fade. This takes time. Beth, don't fight the anger and don't fight the sadness. All these emotions that you feel are important in helping you adjust to death.

These are emotions that you will have to face, too, Michael, when the time comes. Right now you're displacing anger at your grandmother and your parents and other people for being insensitive to your feelings. They may be unaware of your feelings. What is important for both of you and for any kids who have to face the loss of someone meaningful in their lives is to realize how emotions run wild. You will feel hurt, guilt—could you have done more?—why weren't you a better kid?—why didn't you say the things you should have said?—because with every death there's going to be unfinished business for those left behind. Actions that were not taken and words left unspoken are what is left.

In every life there are bad times and there are good times. There are also in-between times. When the grieving is finally over, you can live comfortably and happily, knowing that for whatever time you had with that person, you were loved and did love. That's truly what counts.

The tough question:

"What can I do about making friends?"

"Silence when I go past. Then laughing. I don't want to walk alone. I'd like some friends. Not many, just one would be OK."

Mark
Sixteen years old
Major interests: Science; sports; girls.

Mark's parents have full-time jobs. After school, until his mother returns from work, Mark assumes responsibility for his younger brothers.

"Next year it should be a lot easier," said Mark. "My mom is changing shifts, which means she won't expect me to be home right after school. Not that it matters much. I really haven't any friends to hang out with.

"I wonder if it's me or something. I don't have friends at school. I'm an outsider. I know it; the other guys know it. I got the message. The guys don't miss a beat letting me know that I don't belong. Sometimes I wish I could go to a school where all the kids came from my kind of background. Maybe it would be easier on me. My dad doesn't see why I don't have any friends. I get real bothered when he begins the lecture, 'When I was your age, I had buddies. What's up kid?' When I hear him say this, I boil over inside. Big deal. So he was a helluva lot better than me. He had friends.

"My mom says I should try being nicer to the other guys, and they'll respond. What does she mean? Buy them off? Little she knows. I do well in school. I'm not tops by any means. Let's put it this way. I'm better than OK. If I was a genius, it wouldn't matter, I guess, that I don't have friends. But I'm no genius. I know pretty well who I am, and I can't see what's so wrong. I think I'm a decent person. I get good grades. I go to mass. I say prayers.

"I'm not trying to talk about myself like I was some kind of saint. No way. It's just that I'm not a troublemaker. That's true. My parents don't get called from school about my behavior. I get this feeling that I've made myself sound like I'm some kind of nothing. Maybe that's my problem. But I don't see myself like that. Who would? All I know is I don't get calls from friends and I don't have anyone I can call.

"I hear guys always talking about plans for big Saturday nights. They'll be in the hall in groups, the guys, I mean, and I come down the hall and turn the corner. The guys are in a huddle. Someone sees me coming. The huddle gets smaller and tighter, and then there's that silence until I pass. I keep on walking, trying to pretend I don't see or hear what's going on.

"When I go past, I hear laughing but I don't turn around. I only wish I could make myself walk taller, shoulders up, you know, like I was some football or basketball star. But that doesn't happen. I stay hunched over and even try to make myself smaller and smaller, like I was going to disappear. I wait and then turn the corner down another corridor before I lift my head.

"I've tried to talk to someone about how I feel, and all this person said to me was to keep on walking alone. 'You'll walk further in life than any of those creeps you want as friends.' I honestly don't know what that means. Besides, all of those guys aren't creeps. All I know for sure is that I don't want to walk alone. I want friends. That doesn't seem like a heck of a lot to ask. Not many. One would do me just fine."

The tough answer:

Yes, Mark, we agree. A friend or a chum, whatever you want to call it, is important when you're a teenager. As nice as parents can be, they are not your companions. So we agree with you about the importance of having at least one friend.

The first part of our tough answer is that we're going to urge you not to think that people in the halls are talking about you. Chances are you're the furthest thing from their minds. You'd be surprised how most people are into themselves, in their own worlds, and could care less about you. The point is, we don't want you to become paranoid, imagining all sorts of looks, glances or whatever.

Now with that out of the way, let's focus on what you can do to promote, and what you may be doing to prevent, friendships. It's a pretty harsh thing to ask you right now if, perhaps, you are behaving in ways that keep people from approaching you. Are you sending out signals: not answering, looking away, avoiding others, saying in some way through what you do or how you look that you really don't want others to get close to you?

This may possibly be the case, so we're going to suggest to you that you think about your behavior. Are there things that you do to avoid being with kids your age? Are you interested in what kids your age are interested in doing? Are you purposely trying to be different? Now don't get us wrong. We're not telling you that you should start trying to act, dress or behave differently just so you can win some pals. However, are you purposely trying to be very different just for difference' sake? It's worth thinking about. Oh, by the way, we know it's not easy when your dad says what he says. Your dad cares, and though he might not be expressing his feelings the way you'd like, remember that sometimes it's hard for parents to see negative things happening in their kids' lives—things that they are unable to control.

And now let's think about what you can do. Mark, you have to realize—and really understand this—that friends don't come out of thin air—there has to be a basis for the friendship. This sounds very pompous, doesn't it? Sorry about that. The point is, you have to have something in common with another person or what will you talk about, what will you do together? Right now, you look at guys who have friends, and it all seems mysterious to you. But if you would stop and think about it for a moment, you would realize there's a basis or a reason why those guys are relating.

What about you? What can you do? Let's take your interest in science. We're very sure that there are guys around your school who share this interest, who have questions about science, who talk about science, guys with whom you could speak. Then you would have a basis for hanging out together.

You like sports. There have to be guys interested in the *same* sports that you are. These are the people with whom you won't have to think about what you're going to say. You'll know what to say.

And last but not least, you're interested in girls. Come on, Mark, we know there are plenty of guys in your school who share this same interest and with whom you would have something to talk about. All we want to get across to you is that you have to be willing to share, and you have to see that friends have to have something in common, or there's no point to the friendship. You may not find exactly one person who can share all of your interests. You may end up relating to different people.

It's important that you stay open and forget about the idea of a friend. Instead, we want you to think about what you may have in common with another person, shared interests that will provide you with the opportunity to talk to someone.

We also want to end our tough answer by reassuring you, Mark, that while it is true that we all need a buddy or a friend at some point in our lives, we don't want you to suffer and feel as if you're an oddball. That is far from the case. It simply takes some of us longer to learn how to relate to others. Sometimes in life we will have no choice other than to walk alone, and when that happens we want you to walk with your head high, "six feet tall." Your turn will come, Mark. There will be that buddy, and you'll discover him or her when you are less self-conscious about yourself.

The tough question:

"Is it possible to really communicate with your parents?"

We met with a group of teenagers, and these are just a few of the comments from our discussion about communicating with parents.

"My parents turn a deaf ear when I try to tell them anything they don't want to hear."

"Mom sometimes listens. She really likes to lecture me."

"My dad thinks I'm still a kid. He picks up his newspaper when I try to talk to him about something that's really bugging me."

"Why won't they hear me out? I know they're my parents, but they don't have all the answers."

"It doesn't make me happy, cutting them out from my life. What else can I do if they've got their minds made up that what I'm doing spells trouble? I wish I could just get them to talk to me instead of giving me lectures."

The tough answer:

Teenagers generally agreed that they very much wanted to communicate with their parents, but that they often felt blocked.

"I say something and then my mom gets mad and it's the end of our talking," said Alex. Elizabeth said the reverse was true for her. "Usually, it's my mom or my dad who say something that makes me explode or just get up and walk out of the room."

Whatever the reason, when it comes to emotionally charged topics, parent-teenager discussions all too often get blocked. "I can't tell you how often I've told my mom and dad not to interfere in my life," commented Doreen. "They accuse me of being disrespectful."

"My dad," said Mickey, "tells me I'm getting big ideas, and as long as he's supporting me and I'm living under his roof, I'm going to damn well listen to what he has to say."

Parents can dig their heels in just like you, and then relationships become tugs-of-war. Of course, there are many super times when everything is great between you and your parents—happy, warm, loving family togetherness. Unfortunately, there are also times when communications break down, and these times can leave lingering bad feelings.

In making the leap from teenager to adult, you need

your parents. They can be a great help. You, in turn, can make their lives more meaningful. All throughout this book, we've talked about how teenagers feel that they are old enough to be treated in an adult fashion. But the bottom line is, if you are to be treated as an adult, then you have to behave like one. What does this mean for communication?

First, when you get into a hassle with your parents and the doors slam, or you storm out of the house, or no one talks to anyone at the dinner table, have you ever thought of being the *first* to break the vicious cycle? Being the one to take the initiative and to start opening up lines of communication takes a lot more strength than digging one's heels in and stubbornly staying silent.

In reopening talks with your folks about any subject, don't accuse, don't blame them. Don't send up red flags like, "Dad, you never listen to me. Mom, you are always criticizing me." This isn't war. There's no need to attack first, because when someone attacks, the other person becomes defensive.

Just think about it. "Mom you never listen to me." You've attacked her. What do you expect her to do? "Yes, son/daughter, it's true, I never listen." Of course not. She will open up her own attack.

So let's drop the attack style. A simple, straightforward, "I really would like to talk to you," will help you achieve your goal, which is to communicate with your folks.

Now the hardest part. If your folks have another viewpoint, you've got to listen. Give them a chance to be heard. We know that if you do, the great majority of parents will be happy to hear you out. Without any fancy talk, be straightforward. "I'll listen to you. Please listen to me."

Parents of teenagers hunger for respect. They're kind of fearful that respect is flying out the window as their kids "take wings" and find a whole slew of outside interests and friends. You may not believe us, but it's true when we say how much parents want to feel that their values and their beliefs have had some effect on your life.

If you haven't talked openly and honestly with your parents about sensitive topics, go slowly at first. You just can't plunge into a discussion about serious matters. Practice with small beginnings. Work up to the big questions. It may be that you won't be able to talk to them about some troubling things, and then you will have to turn to other authorities. That's when counselors at your school, your priest or a respected teacher can point you to the right direction.

However, giving your parents a chance to be the first ones to come to your side, providing guidance and insight into life, is crucial. No one will care as much about you as your parents. Give them a chance and listen to them in a reasonable, calm, adult way. Enjoy the surprise and pleasure of watching them develop into mature parents of a well-adjusted teenager, at the same time that you are developing into a mature, responsible, happy adult.

13

The tough question:

"What if I don't want to do what my friends are doing?"

"It's a tug-of-war for me. The pull is strong. When everyone around me, like the guys I hang out with, take drugs, how do I stay clean?"

Benjamin
Seventeen years old
Major interests: Sports; girls; some school subjects; getting into college.

"It's not so easy trying to hack it alone. My friends tell me, 'What's the big deal?' No one is on hard drugs. Right now it's just marijuana and stuff like that. I can't just leave my friends. That's not so easy. I like the guys, but I'm worried. My mom would kill me if she had any idea what's going on."

(More often than not, drug habits begin with pressure from friends. In Benjamin's case, he felt unable to escape his friends' influence. They were in all his classes and lived in the same neighborhood. "It's easy for people to say to me, 'Stay away.' They're not me. I like my friends."

Cindy faces a similar problem. The importance of friends' opinions is causing her a great deal of conflict.)

> *"I know right from wrong. That doesn't help. I made the mistake of letting my best friend know I never had sex. She's not my best friend anymore. She told everybody."*
>
> *Cindy*
> *Fifteen years old*
> *Major interests: Piano; dancing; dating.*

"I really am scared of having sex. I don't like everybody knowing that I haven't. Now my friend's brother teases me. I'm so worried that it's going to get around school. I am so mad at my girlfriend. She had no right to tell. She swore she would keep my secret. I don't want to be different from my friends. I think, sometimes, maybe I should have sex, so I'd be like all the other girls."

"The girl I love wants me to drink. She likes the buzz in her head. I don't want to give in. I like her so much."

Doug
Sixteen years old
Major interests: My girlfriend; football; bringing home good grades for my parents.

"My girlfriend doesn't understand. She thinks I'm a jerk because I won't drink like the other guys. I don't want to drink. I don't even touch a can of beer. She doesn't know that I don't want to go through what my dad went through. My mom went through hell for a long time. My dad is OK now, but it hasn't been easy. My girlfriend is beautiful. She's everything a guy could want. I feel happy with her. The only problem is that she likes to drink. At parties she can drink a six-pack and not even get a buzz. I don't know what to do—how not to drink and still keep the relationship."

(Staying off drugs, steering clear of alcohol, abstaining from sex are typical of some of the dramatic peer pressures that teenagers experience. In the next example, we'll hear from Connie. The pressure she feels about clothing, although *far* less dramatic and with a lot less far-reaching effect, can nonetheless be very emotionally traumatic.)

"It really gripes me that all my friends have beautiful clothes. I feel so different."

Connie
Sixteen years old
Major interests: My appearance; volleyball; English literature.

"I really try, but nothing I buy seems right. I mean, I don't look like the other girls. I don't like my body. I don't like the way I look. My mom says she's not going to keep buying me clothes just because I tell her everybody has a certain kind of outfit and I don't. She doesn't understand how important it is. Like for instance, right now everybody has these funky kinds of shoes, and I want them, too. There's always something. My girlfriend has never worn the same outfit to school twice in a month. I wish I were like her. Her mom understands. Mine doesn't. Can you imagine, my mom told me that if I'm neat and clean that's enough?"

The tough answer:

Others having sex; taking drugs; drinking six-packs; wearing the latest fashions—peer pressure in the teenage years is something you have to cope with. It may be important for you to realize that the peer pressure you're experiencing doesn't begin in the teen years. Remember when you were five years old and some child got a new three-wheeler or some other toy high on your list, and you didn't? Remember how disappointed you were?

Peer pressure starts from the very first day of a child's awareness that he or she isn't the only one in the world, and that there are other kids the same age. We're always subject to pressures. Some have more money than we do; some do better than we do in school; some are prettier, handsomer, have more dates or play a better game of ball. Sometimes you may set the standards. Other times they will be set by someone else. *Escape from peer pressure is just not possible.*

Some peer pressure isn't all that bad. Let's say you hang out with friends who do well in school. The pressure from your peers can motivate you to try harder. Peer pressure is usually thought of in negative terms; however, it can work *for* and not **against** you.

Let's, however, consider negative peer pressures because these are the ones that cause heartaches or problems. What you probably forget is that you have the power to take charge of your own life. Your peers aren't doing anything but being what they are. The pressure comes from *inside your own head.* For example, other girls are having sex but you aren't, Cindy. Well, maybe they are or maybe they are just big talkers. You have to be the one to decide your *own values.* Don't blame the others. They can say what they want. They can't force you to engage in an activity that goes against your own value system.

Doug, you have a girlfriend who wants you to drink. We applaud your decision not to drink. You've 'been there' with a dad who did drink. You had better start now clarifying your position. Sure, you're crazy about this girl and you don't want to lose her. But, keep in mind, if you lose your own values you won't respect yourself, and we can bet that the relationship won't last. Your girlfriend will respect you more for *holding fast to your own values.* Sometimes explanations of your values may be necessary to clarify your stand against drinking.

The message we want to get through to all of you loud and clear is the importance of being true to yourself. Remember, no one can force you to do something. It's not a matter of going around proclaiming to everyone that you don't use drugs, you don't have sex and you don't want to drink yourself into a stupor. It's simply doing what you think is morally correct. And holding to your decisions.

As we noted, peer pressure began a long time ago in your life, only perhaps you didn't call it peer pressure. You called it getting what your friend got for his or her birthday. And peer pressure, that is, awareness of what your peers have or are doing, is going to **continue the rest of your** *life.* As a teenager, it's time to start learning how to select appropriate values, how to find new friends if necessary, how to hold your head high when everyone around is throwing verbal poison darts at you about your behavior. It's a time to put on blinders, if necessary.

Now it is true that teenagers—and people of any age—need buddies. However, the selection process for buddies must be as careful as the selection process for what you will or will not do to conform. We also know that learning to get along with other people is very important in our society. We need other people and other people need us.

However, we have an obligation to ourselves to be selective; so if one group doesn't work out, we're free to shift groups. The first step is knowing your own values and being true to yourself. Next comes saying to yourself, "This group isn't working for me. It's time to move on." No fanfare, no "holier than thou" kind of stance; just a quiet shift is necessary. Never forget, there are plenty of other kids around who share your values, so if one group doesn't work out, others are available.

An important part of growing up is knowing who you are, knowing your values and recognizing similarities and differences among your friends. It's up to you to pick and choose. You can't do anything about the behavior of your friends, but you sure can make decisions about yourself. Make these decisions and hold steadfast.

"My trust and faith in God are gone. What should I do?"

"It's so beautiful—my grandma's belief in God and the church. I envy her trust. I fight an uphill battle with my feelings."

Maureen
Seventeen years old
Major interests: Reading; cheerleading squad; the prom.

Maureen, seventeen years old, talked about her early belief and trust in God. "I had this trust in God. Somehow I believed that if I prayed long and hard enough, everything would turn out just fine. It seemed to work for me. I didn't even feel that I had to talk about my faith. It was so much a part of me. And now it's all gone."

Maureen's life these past several years has been rough. After months and months of squabbling, her father deserted the family and her mother filed for a divorce. Within three months after the divorce, her mother remarried and moved to a different neighborhood from where Maureen had grown up. Two younger brothers went to live with their mother. Not wanting to transfer schools in her senior year, Maureen decided to stay with her grandmother, a devoutly religious woman in her late seventies.

"She's really easy to live with, kind of old, but in some ways she's really cool. My friends think she's kind of cute. She always asks about their boyfriends and makes jokes. She has tons of friends, all ladies from church who look after her. Someone is always stopping over at the house. I go to mass with her and I know how much it means to her that I go. I have decided that it won't hurt me to give up some time since she's always so worried about me and makes sure I have a good supper and stuff like that.

"In church I'll sit next to her, going through the motions of listening and saying prayers, but I have this feeling, you know, like I'm a stranger performing, not me, Maureen, doing all this.

"I look at my grandmother next to me, and I am really freaked out because her face has such a glow, like she's in another world. I have to admit I choke up seeing how she looks. And I know it's not a "put-on" with her. I mean she never says to me like how much she believes and all that. She really does believe in the church. You'd have to see her to know what I mean, like her hands are folded and her face is all relaxed and I swear even the wrinkles seem to go away. I was sure once that she had the face of a young woman. It must have been a trick of the light. I was stunned. I once asked her to tell me what she felt, and she just squeezed my hand and said, "Happiness and joy."

"I don't want to upset her, but I've wanted to ask her about this faith. I'm not sure she could explain. You see, I'm bothered. *I don't feel that way one bit. I don't trust God anymore. I don't trust prayers.* I just have to look at my family for proof. Prayers got us nowhere. My parents divorced, and I'd been praying for a long time that they'd stay together. I had this feeling that I was praying out my heart, and God tuned out and turned off. He never heard what I had to say. I began to tell myself how stupid I was, asking God for favors. I mean, maybe if I were six years old it would be different.

"In a way, I have to admit that I really do feel kind of sad losing my faith. Ever since I can remember, my faith had always been something I could hold on to. No matter what happened, it was just there—a part of me. Now that it's gone, there's a terrible emptiness and I'm going through an awful time of doubting. Deep down, I don't want to lose my faith. I want to hold on to it because it is a lifeline, like climbing some mountain and you need a rope to pull you up. I'm thinking about the bad times and the bad things that happened to me with my parents. If only I could share the trust and belief in God that my grandmother feels, I believe that somehow my life could take a better turn. I don't think that's ever going to happen for sure."

The tough answer:

First of all, Maureen, we think it's great that you can appreciate your grandmother's faith. We really mean this. It would be just as easy for you to discount how your grandma feels—the feelings of an old lady. Now with respect to her faith, we know exactly what you're talking about. We, too, have often seen older people at mass, their faces truly transformed, radiantly happy, as if they had some special secret or communion with God.

We also know that a lot of teenagers like yourself and, for that matter, plenty of adults, feel as if they've lost their faith. We know it's not unusual for someone to be sitting at mass and have lots of distracting thoughts pop into their heads. We once surveyed some teenagers after mass and asked them if they would tell us what they had been thinking about in church. One boy told us that even though he tried stopping himself, all that was on his mind during mass was an afternoon soccer game he was scheduled to play. He said he had really made an effort to think about what was going on, but had had no luck. In fact, it was kind of funny. The harder he tried to think about religion, the more soccer moves popped into his mind. Another teenager told us the only reason he had gone to church that Sunday was because he was trying to get up the courage to ask a girl from his class out on a date. He knew she went to church on Sunday, and so he had suddenly "found" religion.

A girl your same age, Maureen, admitted that *her* thoughts were about an afternoon shopping trip. Her mom said that if she came to mass they would go right from church to the mall. There was a great sweater on sale.

Then we asked these same kids a second question. What did these teenagers think other people were thinking? Each and everyone was sure everyone else was thinking lofty, holy thoughts, and that they were the only ones hampered by earthly concerns. It's simply not the case. What people think about during a church service can differ. The challenge for each and every person, however, is to develop a true and strong relationship with God.

We think one of the problems that stops people from achieving this relationship is trying to bargain with God. In our search for faith, we start off by praying for favors and setting up contracts: "OK, God, I'll believe in you if you do such and such. If you don't come across with what I ask for, I'm going to doubt my faith." Two dolls for Christmas, a toy train, a soccer win, the new sweater, a date with a special girl, parents not divorcing—people, young and old, negotiate contracts on any and all levels.

That's exactly what happened in your case. You lost your faith and trust in God because you bargained with God and God didn't come across with a payoff. In spite of all your well-intentioned prayers, your parents divorced. It was only natural that you felt that God let you down. You thought prayers, especially a prayer like yours, should have God's ear. And since things didn't turn out that way, you became angry, and your faith no longer seemed important to you. God didn't listen to you so why should you listen to God?

We think you are the one who isn't listening because faith is a *gift* of God, not the other way around. Your faith was based on a payoff system. You do this, God, and I'll believe in you. You are bargaining. But that's understandable. It's very human to pray for favors. It takes a lot of weight off our shoulders. We may want a great watch for Christmas, and a little prayer, we'd like to believe, will help fulfill that wish.

In our opinion, your question is *right at the heart of one of the biggest problems that all of us face—the search for faith.* We all need something to believe in so that, no matter what problems come in our way we have something to make sense of the world when it turns upside down or when things go wrong in our personal lives.

We'd like to suggest to you that perhaps the best way to achieve faith is *not* to try too hard. That's a big problem we all have—trying too hard and trying to figure out reasons for believing. Perhaps another way to achieve faith is to get rid of all those bargaining traps we discussed earlier. We honestly feel that the real route to achieving true faith, or as you put it Maureen, restoring your faith, is to let yourself be *open* to believing without bargaining. It's interesting to note that sometimes, when we desperately try for something we want, it doesn't happen. Stepping aside and having a "laid back" attitude helps us to get some perspective. We see everything in a different light.

One sixteen-year-old girl described her experiences singing in a choir. For the most part she worried about the words, the way she looked, the way she breathed. In other words, she tried hard to make sure everything was done exactly right. Occasionally, and she describes these times as very special, she was "into the music." As she commented, "I was completely unaware of myself until afterward. The music was just inside of me, part of me." And, those were the times, she remembers, singing like she never sang before.

We heard of another teenager, a runner, talk about that "moment of truth" as he called it. Usually, when he ran, he worried about how he was doing—were his feet hitting the ground right or were his arms moving the way they should? And then there were times when he ran like the wind, completely forgetting himself, totally unselfconscious and only experiencing the grand and glorious feeling of running.

It's that way, we think, with faith. If you sit and overanalyze your feelings, the achievement of faith becomes a struggle. The trick is to leave yourself *open* to get the gift of faith *from* God. It's not always going to come. Frankly, when you are fifteen, sixteen, seventeen, or whatever, personally experiencing the faith that you observe in your grandmother may not happen for you, at least for the time being.

This does make sense. Your generation has learned to demand proof for everything; thus, you may even seek a scientific basis for your belief. Grandmothers and grandfathers, on the other hand, have done a lot of living and a lot of experiencing. They have the insight to realize that *not* everything in life requires scientific proof.

Don't expect too much from yourself. Frankly, less effort on your part will have a bigger payoff. But then, too, don't get into that pitfall of bargaining with God. God is not a business contractor. "Do this, God, and I'll do that. Give me an A in math, a passing grade in biology, a decent score on the SATs, a date with the right girl and I'll show you, God. I'll believe." Be open; that's all you can reasonably ask of yourself for now. Don't shut down; remember that the gift of faith is from God to you, not the other way around. You can block the process if you try too hard and if you let too much analyzing get in the way. Back off a bit and don't think of your indifference as a loss—ever. That's all you can reasonably ask yourself. There will, we promise, come a "moment of truth," when you'll feel as if you're running like the wind and believing. You will not have searched. *Faith and trust in God will come to you.*

The tough question:

"How can I learn to relate to the opposite sex?"

"I've never once, not once, been asked out on a date. Can you imagine how I feel?"

Janis
Sixteen years old
Major interests: Piano; writing poetry; fun clothes; being asked out on a date.

"All of my girlfriends date. Well, almost all of them. I think I'm the only one who doesn't. During lunchtime it hurts a lot to sit there listening to them talk about their dates. I hate myself because I'm jealous. I feel the jealousy in my stomach, and I don't even want to have lunch. Sometimes I leave, pretending I have homework to do so I won't have to listen, and I won't have to be asked about boys. But no one asks because they know I don't date. I told my mom once that no boy has ever asked me out. "Someday," she told me, "it will happen." Oh how I hate hearing that. Someday. How does she know?

"Maybe I'm not asked out because the boys know I won't have sex with them. I never said I wouldn't, and I don't intend to, but boys kind of know, don't they? I don't know how they know. Maybe I'm lying to myself that this is how it has to be. Maybe it's true. All I know is what's happening to me. If I were ugly, I could understand. I truly would. There's this awful looking girl in my class who has dates. I feel so mean saying she's ugly. I am not telling the truth, am I?

"I'm kind of mixed up. It's just that I was home the night of the junior prom. I watched TV with my dad and went to bed early. I don't think I slept much. Would *you* feel like sleeping on the night of the junior prom if you weren't going and you were home with your parents? They were trying to be nice, but that made it even worse.

"Boys have it so easy. They're the ones who ask. They don't have to sit and wait. I've never once been asked on a date. I don't think anyone in the whole, wide world can imagine how bad I feel."

(Janis has never been asked out and feels the torment of not being like other girls in her class. Although in our culture girls usually have to wait to be asked out, dating is not as easy for teenage boys as girls might imagine. Andy, seventeen, talked about the problem he has—being rejected when he asked a girl out.)

"Last year I asked this girl out. She laughed at me. Sure, I got burned. Wouldn't you?"

Andy
Seventeen years old
Major interests: Band; hanging out with friends; getting into a good college.

"I asked her out for the junior prom. She sat next to me in class, and I thought she kind of liked me. Otherwise I wouldn't have asked. It hurt a lot, you know. It hurt worse because she went to the prom with a buddy of mine. I don't know why she laughed. She stood there at her locker laughing at me. I asked her what was so funny. She didn't answer. I didn't get it. I can't even remember what I said.

"I had this cramped feeling going home, like my stomach, you know, was upset. Dumb, isn't it? I mean feeling this way. It seems all my friends ask girls out and it's no big deal. The one time I ask a girl out, she gives me the cold shoulder, and it hurts a lot. I never saw myself as any great shakes. I really don't much like the way I look. I guess I like myself even less now, after what happened. I tried to forget about it but it's not as easy as you think. I was glad she wasn't in any of my classes this year.

"I worry sometimes about who she told. I passed her the other day, and I was going to trip her on the stairs. It's not easy to forget something like this. I didn't go to the prom. I stayed home. My mom and dad don't know. They offered to pay for everything. My mom said, "Why not ask someone? There must be some girl in your class you could ask." How could I face mom and tell her I asked one girl and she laughed at me. I guess once you're burned, you stay burned."

The tough answer:

How well we understand Andy and Janis. In Andy's case the pain of rejection is like a stab in the back, isn't it? We won't even try to explain the laughter. Did she really laugh, Andy? Or was your imagination running wild because you were being rejected? In the tension of the moment you might have misinterpreted what happened. We are not trying to defend her. We just want to make sure you are going to put this incident in its proper perspective.

The same for you, Janis. Everyone is having a wonderful time on Saturday night but Janis. The only reason you aren't having a good time is that you think you have sent out messages to the boys that you won't have sex.

The real truth is that all your friends may or may not be having dates. All your friends may or may not be dashing to the prom. When some very disappointing things happen to us in life, we take comfort in making up stories to help us feel better. We come up with all sorts of excuses or rationalizations, like girls are dumb or boys are only after sex, and there's absolutely nothing wrong with this first stage of comforting ourselves. Why shouldn't we do what we can to make ourselves feel better about unfortunate or unpleasant events?

However, after this important initial stage of comforting, we must move on. ***Rationalizations or excuses can be self-defeating.*** We think both of you and other kids who have had similar experiences should be enjoying a great social life and have the opportunity to date. And we don't want you, Andy, to be turned off by rejection.

There are bound to be many times in life when all of us experience rejection. No one, and we don't care who they are, always wins, is always triumphant, is always accepted.

Rejection isn't our idea of fun. It can be very painful. It makes you want to crawl in a hole and hide away to soothe your injured spirit.

But after this period "in the pits," it's time to pick up the pieces of your life and charge on. That's what you have to do, Andy. You have to learn from the rejection. You must not let one girl's refusal keep you in a tailspin—absolutely not. Of course it hurt terribly, and you may not forget it for a while.

Later on, you might think back a bit, and in a cool, unemotional way reflect on what happened. Was this girl really right for you? Had she already accepted the other boy's invitation and was embarrassed and stunned to be asked to the same affair by his friend? We would like to think there is some explanation for her behavior other than being mean-spirited. Had you ever related to this girl before you asked her out to the prom? You know, your invitation might have come "out of the blue." We just don't want you to be swept away by the emotions of the situation, so much so that you distort what happened.

Janis, you, too, must not let yourself be tormented by not being asked out. Of course it is painful. Of course you feel awful. You say that boys just want sex, and that's why you aren't asked out. Remember what we said to Andy. Sometimes in life, when things aren't going the way we want them to, we make up stories. You may have made up a story. We're not saying that sexual attraction isn't important. We are just saying that you can't be sure that all boys only want sex on their dates. That's demeaning to boys. Some boys do, perhaps, but then you don't want to date those boys anyhow.

Right now both of you, like so many other teenagers, feel that you just don't have the social life that you'd like. At this point, your best strategy is to think about things that will enhance your self-respect, not tear it down. A whole new approach for both of you, we feel, would be the best solution. First and foremost, we'd like you to put dating *completely out of your mind—completely.* Don't react with shock. Just wait a moment and hear our reasoning. Janis, drop all ideas of boys asking you out. Andy, don't dream of inviting a girl to a party or a movie.

What do we want you to do? We want you to start reacting to the opposite sex as people, not as dating objects. Janis, there must be boys at your school who are interested in music. Relate to these boys, share your interests and make sure to share theirs. *Focus on the other person as a person, not as some kind of prize to be won for a Saturday night.*

Andy, the same game plan should apply for you. You mentioned, for example, your concern about getting into a good college. There must be girls in your class who have this same goal. Why not begin talking about what you want to do and where you want to go to school? Listen to *their* hopes and dreams. In other words, we want you to get all of this dating stuff out of your head. When you think of the opposite sex as a person with interests and feelings, a person with whom you have something in common, you'll begin to see each girl as a real human being rather than a prize for an evening. With this new approach, you're bound to succeed in having good relationships with the opposite sex.

We truly believe this. We are not saying that physical attraction isn't important. We are not saying there doesn't have to be some chemistry. We are saying that, for dating to have any basis, there must be something you share. By the way, this kind of viewpoint—seeing the opposite sex as a real person with real feelings—is going to have tremendous importance for you later in life. The foundation of a meaningful, serious relationship is mutually shared interests. There's no better place or age to begin than in the teen years.

We promise you, Janis and Andy, that if you follow our suggestions, relationships will fall naturally in place. There will be laughter and friendship, along with the sharing of an evening's fun and games. And, as a footnote, we have to let you in on a secret we have discovered in our discussions with teenagers. While you may believe right now that everyone else but you is confident, secure, happy, poised, attractive and dating like mad, we've discovered that 99 percent or more of teenagers go through long periods when they think that they are all arms and legs, clumsy and unsure. Of course there will be occasions when everything is out of joint and unpleasant, but these times do serve a purpose. It makes the happy times sweeter, and the happy times, we know, are what will remain in your life's memory bank.

16

"What should I do when my parents have problems?"

"My dad pretends it doesn't matter, but I know inside it's driving him crazy that he lost his job."

Paul
Seventeen years old
Major interests: Baseball; what college I'm going to apply to; hanging out with my friends.

"My dad isn't the same guy he was a year ago. I can't get him to come to a game. It's like he doesn't want to be with people. He lost his job because his company downsized. He was dumped. He said that a younger guy was hired for less money. To be honest, I never thought much about my dad's work. I mean, like I didn't have all that much interest. He didn't talk much about what he did. Now all I can think about is that job. Mom's paycheck covers family expenses.

"The thing that really got to me, and the thing I can't shake loose from, was the morning I saw my dad crying. Not crying like a kid, you know, just his voice shaking and his eyes kind of funny. He was talking about what happened at the company. It really got to him, being let go after twenty-five years. I feel pretty guilty because I was upset and went to school. I didn't think about what had happened to him, really. It hadn't registered with me. It's not like I didn't care—more like I didn't want to hear about what happened. I still really don't want to know."

> *"I'm American. My parents aren't. Having foreign parents is no fun."*
>
> *Alex*
> *Sixteen years old*
> *Major interests: Soccer; chemistry; making the honor society.*

About six years ago, Alex's family immigrated to America. Alex feels lucky because he was young enough to adapt to a new country. "When no one speaks your language, you learn fast. At home, my parents speak Croatian. They say it's good for me to have two languages, but I'm not so sure. I don't argue with them. My mom refuses to learn English. She can't even go to the store by herself.

"Neither of my parents fit into the American way of life. They're always comparing life here and in Croatia. I ask them, 'Why did you come if it's so rotten here?' They never answer. They say something like they thought it would be better in America. I don't remember if everything was so great like they say. But, that's not the way they talk.

"They're always saying it was better over there, and that makes problems for me, like my mom not wanting me to dress like American kids. She's worse with my sisters. All three of us, my two sisters and me, are beginning to resent them. I feel terrible saying this, but what can I do? I feel split down the middle. I like my school. I like my life.

"My problem is not with America. My problem is with my parents' having problems. Whenever I hear about the great, 'old country,' I feel like telling them to go back there and leave me here. I wish they would be more American. I feel embarrassed sometimes about the way my mom looks. Please don't tell me I'm a bad, disrespectful son. I know that they're trying their best for me to have a better life. I don't want to feel sorry for them. I feel sorry for me."

> *"My mom is getting married. Her marriage to my dad was annulled. I feel so hurt and bitter, and I hate the idea of calling an old man with gray hair 'Dad.' Mom said if I keep fighting her, she'll make me live with my real dad."*
>
> *Nicole*
> *Fourteen years old*
> *Major interests: My cat; good grades; dancing classes.*

"My dad lives in California. I don't know anyone there. All of my friends are in New Jersey. I'll go there in the summer, but I don't want to change schools now. Besides, he's married and there's a new baby there. My mom and I were always best friends, but it's all turned around now. She's getting married, and she wants me to call this man, 'Dad.' He's terrible. He isn't mean to me or anything like that. He's just not my real dad. Mom can't get this through her head. He has two kids of his own, and I'm supposed to act like they're my relatives. I don't even want to know them. They're a lot older and away at college. It will just be me and my mom with this man, living together.

"Sometimes, when I go to sleep at night, I close my eyes and I see my dad, my real dad, and my mom in the backyard. We're having a barbecue the summer before they split. My mom turns on the sprinkler; we're all getting wet and not caring. I'm laughing and not even cold.

"The wedding is soon. I think about falling down and breaking my leg or something because I don't want to go. And then there's Mom telling me, 'You have to shape up' young lady. Dave is a great guy. I'm in love with him. If you keep on behaving this way, like it or not, you will have to live with your father.' Is it wrong to hate my mom?"

"Mom has cancer. She's had chemo and supposedly they got all the cancer. The real truth is that with her kind of cancer, no one knows. She's not doing so great."

Martha
Sixteen years old
Major interests: My life is divided into two parts— before cancer—everything—you name it: school, boys, prom. Now—pretty much nothing.

"My mother is very sick. She doesn't let on like she is because she keeps trying to run the house, clean and cook, and she can't do it. I end up helping or doing it myself. I have two younger brothers. No one wants to talk about what's going on. She just says she's a fighter. Dad says she's a fighter. Everyone says this. But personally I think it has nothing to do with fighting. It's in her body, so it doesn't matter what her mind is doing. My life has changed. I think I should drop out of school. Then, other times, I think it's unfair that so much is being dumped on my shoulders."

The tough answer:

Sadness, anger, rage, resentment, hate—the whole range of emotions you kids feel about your parents' problems and their effect on your lives is normal and makes sense. It is unfair that life has dealt these blows—a father losing his job, a mother suffering from cancer, parents unhappy with the failure of America to live up to their expectations, a stepfather who cannot replace a real father. You and other teenagers facing similar problems have a right to feel sorry for yourselves, a right to express disgruntled feelings, and, on occasion, to behave inappropriately.

However, after a while, and we hope that you will keep that time brief, we suggest you call a halt and start putting your lives in order again. Negative feelings give one short-lived satisfaction. They relieve tension. In the long run, however, they're counterproductive. For example, Nicole could have a good knock-down-drag-out verbal battle with her mom and still end up at square one—her mom insisting she call the new husband "Dad."

When one faces parental problems there should be two objectives: one, to make life smoother for yourself, and two, to be helpful to your folks. Wasting valuable time being angry, hurt, resentful, bitter or consumed with hate prevents your accomplishing these goals.

Now, what can you realistically do when parents have problems out of your control but which inevitably spill over into your lives? There are some concrete actions you can take: First, it will be important for you to recognize and truly accept that your parents are individuals just like yourself. You want your parents to respect you as an individual. Don't you agree they deserve the same respect?

Let's consider the situations that you kids pinpointed earlier. Alex, your parents are disappointed with their new lives. Haven't you ever been disappointed? They may feel cheated and concerned about how all of your lives are changing. That's a rough bit of reality to accept when you're older. You saw how easy it was for you to adapt. You were very young. It's a lot easier to adapt to different things when you are a child. You don't have to feel sorry for them, however. We simply suggest that you show them some tolerance and understanding. You can best do this by compromising. Going a small step in small matters may be a giant step forward in easing your parents' concerns.

Anything you kids can do to lighten pressures on your parents, reduce the stresses they are experiencing, will be of enormous value. They have enough problems on their minds. Your goal is not to add to their already filled plate of problems, but to do what you can to relieve their burdens. For example, Paul, of course, it hurts when your dad doesn't want to show up for a game. You're also upset because you saw a bit of frailty in him—almost tears one morning. He's human, just as you are. Haven't you ever felt tearful, even though you were doing your best to keep a macho face turned toward the world? Take cues from your dad. Let him share what's going on in his life if he wants to share. Do what you can to keep your relationship with him uncluttered.

Relieving the pressures on your folks—making some

decisions on your own, doing your best not to add to their burdens—are realistic actions that you can take. Is it wrong to ask teenagers to take such a mature approach? We think not. Will your self-esteem be injured because you compromise? Definitely not. Nicole, for example, can make it clear to her mother that she has a problem calling this new guy in her mom's life, "Dad." Showing respect, making an effort to relate to the man, is far more important than what name he is called. You might even ask your mom how she would feel if you started calling your real dad's new wife, "Mommy."

The consequences of the tolerance, the compromise and the mature behavior that we're suggesting are going to affect you kids. While it is true you will be forced to grow up faster than friends of yours whose parents are not facing similar circumstances, this push into maturity is not all bad. You are being given an unusual opportunity to acquire the special strengths of compassion and sensitivity, a chance to learn how to salvage good from the bad happenings in your lives.

Everybody goes through ups and downs. You kids are just going through these stages at a time in your lives when you'd much prefer to be having fun, hanging out with your friends, enjoying the freedom of being teenagers without adult responsibilities weighing you down. We agree one hundred percent that it would be great if this were the case. However, it isn't. You can't change the situations facing your parents. What you can change, however, is your behavior and your response.

We've made a big point of compromise, compassion and turning the negative into something positive. However, there's still one remaining issue that does concern us, and that is the risk of your being scarred by parental problems. Therefore, although we've stressed empathy, compassion and compromise, *we feel very strongly about your right to have a personal life outside of the home.* This means that it's not a time to close down, to shut yourself away from your friends. This means, that while you are showing sensitivity and compassion toward your parents, you must also do things that are self-replenishing in order to keep a balance in your life. Strong doses of good times with friends, activities in school—these are important. *There is absolutely no need to feel guilty.* Life has many different compartments, and because one aspect of your life is on a downside, it doesn't mean that everything else has to be turned around. Meeting the downside with a positive approach can go a long way toward turning things around for everybody. Obviously not everything can be turned around. All we can realistically expect of ourselves is a sincere effort to try our best.

17

"What can I do about feeling depressed—thinking the worst, like suicide?"

"I can't see things in my life getting any better. I really can't."

William
Seventeen years old
Major interests: Very little of anything right now.

"There are a lot of days when everything goes wrong. The coach is always threatening to kick me off the team. I only have a couple of friends. They don't care much if I hang out with them or not. I can't seem to get anything right. I thought about talking to my mom, but right now she's got a lot on her mind with her dad being sick and all that. I feel bad about him, but I really feel lousy mostly about myself. I don't think my dad would understand. He's not that kind of guy—he's not unhappy or anything like that.

"It seems like nothing was ever right in my life. Well, maybe that's not true. I used to have fun when I was a little kid. What scares me most is, when I'm alone in my room at night and I can't sleep and I'm just staring at the wall, I think about suicide and what it must be like. Maybe the coach would feel guilty. I would like that. There were a couple of suicides in school last year. I didn't know the kids—two of them had some kind of pact, and the teachers told us it was a horrible thing that these kids did, and that none of us should think about doing something like that. It made me think a lot about suicide after that. I wonder if I'm too scared to go that way. But if I did, I wouldn't have these problems, would I, like the teachers not liking me, the coach threatening me all the time, and my world all turned in the wrong direction? I can't see things getting any better. I really can't. I feel stuck, going nowhere. I must be abnormal—a weirdo or something."

> *"If you just looked at me, you wouldn't know that inside I'm all torn up."*
>
> *Anne*
> *Sixteen years old*
> *Major interests: I wish I could think of something.*

"Life is not much fun for me. I can't keep any friends. My mom doesn't know this. She'll ask me about my friends, and I lie to her because I don't want her unhappy. It's the sadness I sometimes feel that lasts like forever. I can't shake it off. Even though you wouldn't think I'm crying if you just look at me, inside I feel that way. Everything around me feels so heavy.

"I can barely make myself get up in the morning and go to school. I think I'm the only person in the whole world who feels this huge weight right on my back. That's when my head starts pounding like nails being driven right into my skull. I have thought a little bit about suicide. I asked a sort of friend of mine if she ever had these thoughts. She looked at me and asked if I was crazy or something.

"Am I crazy? That scares me."

The tough answer:

There are times in everyone's life when the world seems too much to take. We know your first reaction to this opening remark might be, "So what? The fact that other people feel this way doesn't solve my problems."

Of course it doesn't. However, before we go on and talk about your depression, occasional suicidal thoughts and what you can do to help yourself, we felt if you knew that such feelings are not as uncommon as you might have assumed, that you would believe us when we say without a moment's hesitation, "Anne, you're not crazy. William, you're not abnormal or a weirdo."

There isn't a person alive who hasn't at one time or another experienced bouts of depression. The reason you kids aren't aware of this is simply because when one is depressed, there is a closing down, a shutting off of the world and a withdrawal into oneself. People are reluctant to share their depressed feelings with just anybody. Both of you, and any other kid who is depressed, behave in the same way—"shutting down and turning off."

Many things can happen. For example, friends will be rejected. Friends can't enter the world. Parents, too, may be avoided. You may not even feel like talking to anyone. Depression does affect your behavior. You put up walls and stumbling blocks, shutting yourself off from outside contacts. And, because you do this, you feel very much alone and deserted by everybody.

It is going to take strength on both your parts to treat this "impostor" who has taken over your life. Sometimes coping with depression takes a great deal more than mere words, so first, we are going to strongly urge you to make sure that you're in good shape physically. A visit to your doctor is an absolute must.

Second, and equally as important as far as we are concerned, we want to make sure that neither of you—nor others who feel the same way—stay alone or avoid contact with others who count in your life. You must not go into a cocoon and hide from relationships.

And, finally, although we believe that people should take an active charge in managing their own lives and strive to be captains of their destinies as much as possible, we also realize that this approach cannot cover every situation. *There are exceptions,* and depression and extreme anxiety are two of them. *Outside help is an absolute must.* No matter how strong you think you are, in dealing with depression, you really must have advice and guidance.

There's nothing unusual about having fleeting thoughts of suicide and fantasies about how everyone will mourn your passing. That's a very dramatic scenario taking place in your mind, and you are at the center of the drama. However, these thoughts, if they persist, are more than just drama. It's time for you to talk to adult figures in your world.

In this book of tough answers to tough questions, we've been careful to treat you with the maturity you rightfully deserve. We honestly do respect the decision-making power of teenagers and their ability to accept rational advice. We have treated you in an adultlike fashion, because, after all, you are just a stone's throw away from being adults.

In considering the tough problems of depression and suicide, we have the same respect for your ability to behave maturely. However, there is one enormous difference between the tough answer to this tough question and the others we have discussed. *The difference is the absolute unconditional need for you or anyone else who has thought about suicide or been depressed to find appropriate help.*

Who can be most helpful?

1. If your school has a guidance counselor, we urge you to go to that person immediately.

2. Confide and consult with your priest.

3. Speak with a teacher whom you can trust.

4. Do talk to your parents. We know they will have helpful suggestions about how best to handle your problems.

The guidance and caring of experienced adults is critical. Then and only then, with the right support, will you be able to battle this intruder in your life with strength and courage.

"I want to hide sometimes when the arguing begins. There's the slammed door, the car starting and my mom crying. Why can't they divorce?"

Diana
Sixteen years old
Major interests: Dancing; choir practice; the fighting at home to stop.

"I don't know why my mom and dad don't get along. That's the understatement of the century. Honest. My mom has told me my dad is running around with a younger woman from his office. I don't believe it. I asked my dad and he said, 'No.' I believe my dad. He says my mom never understood him and my mom says the marriage was a mistake from the start. She knew after the marriage. Why didn't they break up before they had me and my brothers? If they knew the marriage was all wrong, why were they so stupid as to have kids? I really don't know what to believe.

"They fight constantly. I have two younger brothers, and they never seem to hear my parents arguing. I suppose, if they did, it wouldn't matter anyhow. They could care less. All they care about is baseball. It's different for me. I can have the greatest day at school and not think about what's going on at home, and then comes evening and everything changes. After dinner, if my dad even comes home, they are at each other like wolves. I try to stop them. I ask them to think of us kids. I told them they can't keep screaming at each other. It only makes things worse. My dad never before used bad language at me except when I tried to stop them from fighting.

"He tells me to keep my nose out of something that isn't my business. I yelled back at him that it is my business. The family is being destroyed and I feel so miserable listening to the two of them, especially at night. Now I try not to let on how I feel. It makes Mom cry. She tells me I'm a cold fish. She wants me to take sides against my dad.

"I just want them to stop quarreling and to live together. I remember it was so nice at home when I was a little kid. Now it's hell. I would go and live somewhere else if there was a place that I could go. Anything would be better than broken dishes, the front door slamming, the car motor starting, the car screeching out of the driveway and Mom in the kitchen crying.

"I once thought being a teenager would be fun. Now I count the days until I can leave. It shouldn't be that way. I keep praying it will all change. For sure, no one is answering my prayers.

"What I want to know is, if they don't love each other anymore, if life in our house is hell, then why won't the church let them get a divorce? Nothing could be worse than it is now at home. God can't be so mean as to want everyone in my house to keep on suffering like this. What's so bloody awful about divorce? Don't kids have a right to happiness? The way it is now, it could only get better after a divorce.

"I don't even care if my dad finds another wife and my mom some other guy. I mean half the kids in my class have parents who are divorced. You know what my friend said to me? This was before all this happened in my family. She said to me, 'What's wrong with your parents? They're the only parents of all our friends not divorced or separated.' It was a joke at the time. I felt special 'cause it wasn't happening in my home. I don't feel special anymore."

"I never thought I'd come out and say I hate my parents' guts. I feel like I have a dead weight around my neck. My mom is walking out on my dad. She said she waited until I was old enough. It's not fair, is it? To destroy my life?"

Ron
Seventeen years old
Major interests: Cars; my girlfriend; getting good grades for college applications.

"My mom told me she's leaving my dad—getting her walking papers is how she put it. I hate them for what they're doing to me and my life. My kid sister is moping around.

She tries coming to me for help and I can't help her. I've got enough on my mind. I really feel lousy about all this. My girlfriend says we should run off and get married and get away from them. There are problems in her family, too. It's funny to me 'cause I had no idea that any of this was happening. It's hard going to school with all this in my life."

The tough answer:

We aren't going to take sides, though deep down, Ron and Diana, we cannot hide from the fact that we feel your pain and anger at what's going on. Why it happened in your families, of course, is something we can't answer. Should it have happened? Of course not. Can we change the course of what's going on? Can we urge them to get marriage counseling, to hang in there during the rough spots inevitable in every marriage? Unfortunately not.

However, even if we cannot make a difference in their lives, we can deal with *your* concerns. Let's go back a bit to a point you raised, Diana, about God and the church's feelings about marriage. God can't be so mean as to want to keep two unhappy people bound to each other. What *is* so awful about divorce, as you put it.

What God has joined together let no one separate. (Matthew 19:6; Mark 10:9). Yes, there is a strong basis for church reasoning about divorce. A marriage in God's eyes is something that you just can't break up so easily. It's a lot different from having a boyfriend or a girlfriend, going steady, and then deciding to break off the relationship and going on to the next boyfriend or girlfriend.

The dissolution of a marriage is another story. The church law doesn't mean married couples cannot obtain a civil divorce or live apart, particularly when living together is making both kids and parents completely miserable. The church *in no way* stands in the way of couples obtaining legal divorces.

(By the way, we sometimes talk about God and put words or thoughts in God's mouth and accuse God of being mean or unfair. The one thing we have to make sure of is that the words or ideas we ascribe to God truly are the right ones—not wishes or our own thoughts.)

Now let's talk more about what happens in the case of a legal divorce. Couples who have been married in the church have been joined together by God and cannot be separated unless they obtain an annulment from a church tribunal. An annulment simply means that the marriage is not considered a marriage under church law. Remember, a couple can get a legal divorce but must have an annulment in terms of church law.

Legally divorced persons can marry again in church if they get an annulment. Why the steps? The reality is that divorces are a source of great unhappiness, not only for the husband and wife, but for children as well. Divorces just don't "happen" one day in a couple's life. It's traumatic for everyone concerned. Therefore, church law, recognizing that there are some marriages that will never work, follows some carefully thought-out, appropriate steps to make certain that the original sanctity of the institution of marriage endures.

The body of the church, just like any mature, understanding individual person, wants to relate to legally divorced persons in a sympathetic and sensitive manner. It's just that the church requires that before a remarriage can take place, there must be an annulment of the first marriage. Remember, what God has joined together let no one separate.

19

"I didn't know she wasn't Catholic when I fell in love."

Anthony
Seventeen years old
Major interests: Football (all sports); science; my girlfriend.

"My present relationship is pretty overpowering. I'm not a virgin. I wouldn't have sex with this girlfriend. That's how special the relationship is to me. I think she is someone I want to spend the rest of my life with. We plan on going to the same college. Except when we have classes, or I have team practice, we're together. That's the way it is. I've been going with different girls since I was twelve. Maybe I was sexually precocious. That's why I think I know the difference between just a one-night stand, a crush, and the feelings that I have for this girl.

"I honestly had no idea she wasn't Catholic. Now that I think about it, I can understand why I didn't know. I just assumed she was Catholic. She hung out with Catholic kids. She never said anything about not being Catholic. She wasn't hiding anything. We've talked about it and she said she thought I knew she wasn't Catholic. I guess it's just that most kids don't ask this. You just assume, as I did, that everyone in the crowd is Catholic.

"I can't talk to my parents. I want to very much because I need some help. Is it wrong? I try to be rational and tell myself it doesn't matter. But down deep I worry about my mom and my dad and especially my grandmother. That's the one who will blow her top. She has two sons, my uncles, who are priests. If she ever finds out, I know she will work on my mom and my dad to make me break up with this girl.

"My problem and what I want to ask my parents is this: If the girl is beautiful, intelligent and wonderful what difference does her religion make? *Aren't all good people fundamentally the same?*"

The tough answer:

You're right on, Anthony, when you commented, "Aren't all good people fundamentally the same?" Without one moment's hesitation, we agree with you one hundred percent. However, let's first consider your grandmother and your parents, and try to understand where they are coming from. They are concerned, and not wholly without good cause, that when you cross various ethnic, social or religious lines *in a marriage,* there may be problems. Of course, this isn't always the case. However, when one considers marriage, which is a permanent, lifetime relationship, there may be lines that simply can't be crossed.

But the problem you've posed for us is not a marriage, but rather a boy-girl relationship in the teen years. And that's quite another story. It is clear you haven't even discussed the subject with them. That's what frequently happens. Kids tell us that their parents won't listen to them. Now give them a break—give them more credit. We have a hunch, and we could be wrong, that they would agree with us that tolerance in life for various ethnic and sociocultural groups has to begin early in life or it's never learned.

The reality is that our country is a multicultural, multi-everything country. We're not trying to "flag wave" here, but our country's strength does come from differences. And any experiences that you can get relating to people who are different are going to be very important to you in life. Looking at a whole person's value rather than a single attribute of religion, race, or whatever is one of the greatest lessons that you can learn in life.

We would support you and your friends if you continued to associate with different groups in school and outside of school. There is absolutely nothing wrong in relating to kids who may be totally different from anyone you've ever known. In your case, you, yourself, said that the relationship didn't involve sex. This means that you have tons of other common ground, and that is great. That's the way it should be.

At seventeen, you should have fun and games with lots of people. *It's not a time for marriage. It's not a time to "groove" in with one person and convince yourself that this is the person you're going to marry and have a family with.* If this girl is as decent and as wonderful as you say, we believe in your judgment. Enjoy the friendship of *this time and this place.*

You say you can't talk to your parents and you can't talk to your grandmother. You may be very surprised at this, but we urge you to try. We have often discovered that kids have built roadblocks that just don't exist. Now you're going to have to take control here.

We suggest talking to each parent separately. If you do this in a straightforward way, you may be surprised at their calm reaction. More than anything, they're probably desperately worried about whether you are having sexual relations. The thought of your getting a girl pregnant and destroying your future with an unwanted early marriage are just a few of the fearsome possibilities that may be on your parents' minds.

Let them rest easy. Let them know in some way that all you're doing is relating together in a warm, social way. A broad hint to Mom and Dad that sex is *not* on your agenda will make a huge difference. And you may even be more shocked when you discover that your grandmother is not so archaic as you think.

We have a suggestion, and don't laugh or put us down. Try introducing this girl to your grandmother. Grandmothers love attention, and if she sees that this girl is the great companion and the lovely, intelligent and decent person you know she is, you may find that Grandma may even become your biggest ally. I know you think we're joking, but sharing your feelings with your grandmother can be helpful. We're not talking about some melodramatic presentation. All we're saying is this: some afternoon when Grandma is around, and you're with this girl, try a "Hello Grandma, I'd like you to meet a friend of mine." Give the two ladies a chance for a few minutes' chat and see what happens.

The message we want to get across to you, Anthony, and to all teenagers, is that life is more than being with people who think, behave and are carbon copies of ourselves. *A serious relationship involving marriage and kids is another story. Anyway you're not ready for that by a long shot.* Kids use the words "in love." We aren't dismissing or discounting your feelings. But there's a lifetime ahead of you for love and a lasting relationship. Enjoy these teenage moments in time. What is most important now is that you have discovered the fact that fundamentally good people have a lot in common, and that's something really worthwhile to know, not just for you, but for everyone.

"I wish I knew what was going to happen to me in the future."

Peter
Seventeen years old
Major interests: College applications; career; everything about my future.

The tough answer:

"We've now reached the last of our twenty questions, and, as the familiar saying goes, last but certainly *not* least. What's going to happen to you? Is there life after high school graduation? Friends are going to split up and go separate ways. Will you get into college? Maybe you aren't even sure that you want to go to college. What kind of job will you have? Will you have a job? Maybe you don't even know if you want a job or a career. Will you ever fall in love, get married and have kids? Maybe you don't know whether you want to get married and have kids. You may want to just go somewhere and spend your time surfing. Where are you going to live? Do you wish that high school could go on forever? Or maybe you can't wait for high school to end so that you can get on with your life. The only problem is, you haven't the foggiest notion of what that life is.

Lots of doubts and uncertainties about the future begin to haunt you more and more in the teen years, especially as you approach the end of this chapter of your life. Teenage years are special. You aren't quite an adult, and you're certainly not a child. However, there inevitably comes a time when these years wind down and adulthood stares you in the face. The cocoon world of home breaks open. You're ready for adulthood—or are you?

Like Peter, many of you brought up concerns about the future as an important issue. Everybody's curious about the future. That's why there are fortune tellers pretending to know the future; crystal balls, palms to study, fortune cookies with promises, horoscopes—all trying to unravel future mysteries. Unfortunately they are worthless. Nowhere can anyone find a blueprint of one's own destiny. Life unfolds day by day, month by month, and year by year.

Does this mean that worries or concerns about the future must be handed over to fate? Does this mean that you must sit back and take what happens to you in life without any control on your part? Emphatically *no!* In some respects, your future is in your control. You can strive to be captain of your fate and master of your soul. While you may not be able to do anything about the inevitable individual events, there's a lot that you *can* do that will make an enormous difference in how you handle the uncertainties of life.

1. You're going to trust yourself, believe in yourself. Others may not always have the same faith. Others may try to cut you down to size, criticize you unfairly, blame you when you aren't to blame, but if you know in your heart that you're doing the right thing, detractors won't be able to destroy the faith that you have in yourself.

2. You're going to be patient. You can't expect to have everything you hope for, dream about and wish for to happen overnight. Sure, there are lottery winners but you aren't going to waste your time hoping you win the lottery. Buy that lottery ticket if you insist, but, never forget one of life's best allies for achieving your desire is patience.

3. Keep your ambitions, by all means. However, as you charge full speed ahead, don't demean your achievements by having them tainted by malice toward others— by hate, revenge or climbing the ladder to success at someone else's expense.

4. Dare to dream the impossible. For example, dreaming about how great you'd feel with an all-A report card is fine; however, the dream should not be a substitute for honest-to-goodness effort.

5. Learn to walk alone when that is necessary. If the people around you are drinking themselves under the table, taking drugs they shouldn't be taking, engaging in activities you know are morally wrong, hold your head high and keep to your own course. Remember to have faith in yourself, and that faith involves the will to hold on when everyone around you crumbles and gives in to temptations and activities that you know are destructive. At times like these, there's nothing wrong with a healthy dose of egocentricism.

6. Learn to keep your cool when inevitable losses or setbacks occur. No life escapes these ups and downs, these peaks and valleys. In the low times, just coast for a while.

7. Whatever you undertake, give it your best shot. Although you might not succeed, enjoy the satisfaction of knowing you tried your utmost. Rudyard Kipling once wrote, "If you can fill the unforgiving minute with sixty seconds worth of the distance run, yours is the earth and everything that's in it." We strongly agree!

A Final Word:

Keep asking questions. Questions are the first step in helping you to articulate and *identify* the problem.

Keep talking. Dialogue is important. When you hide your feelings and personality from people, then people will not be aware that you need care and support.

Share your fears. It is important to share your fears with someone who cares. Understand that it is OK to have fears—everyone has them.

Seek counsel from "expert" adults. These "experts" can be your parents, clergy, teachers or even books, magazines and encyclopedias.

Trust your own instincts. Seek guidance, but use your own life experience and comfort level to apply solutions that fit you and your personal style.